Math Practice

Reinforce and Master

Basic Math Skills

Grades 1–2

Credits

Author: Janie Schmidt
Production: Quack & Company, Inc.
Illustrations: Carol Tiernon
Cover Design: Peggy Jackson
Cover Credits: Photo www.comstock.com

ISBN 0-88724-936-1

Table of Contents

Table of Contents

Introduction

Math Practice is filled with fun and challenging activities to help students develop and review a wide selection of math skills. Students will practice adding and subtracting, explore time and money, learn basic geometry concepts, identify fractions, and much more. The book is filled with a variety of riddles and puzzles students will enjoy completing. Easy-to-follow teaching elements accompany many of the skills. These elements will help build a mathematical foundation for the students. Review units are included midway and at the end of the book. These units assess the skills practiced. Teachers and parents will find *Math Practice* a valuable tool for helping students achieve growth in their mathematical development.

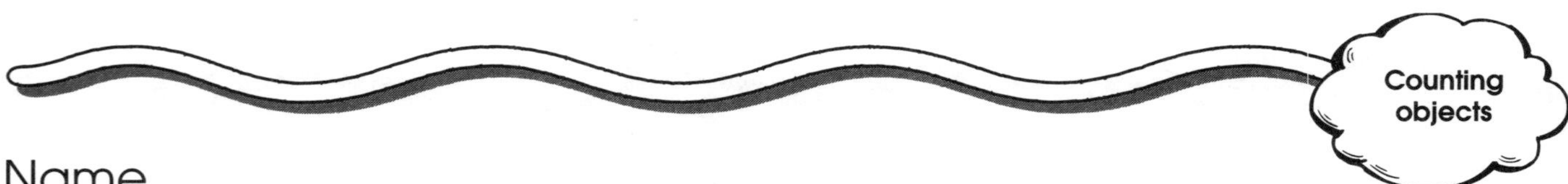

Name ____________________

Bug Bonanza

To keep your place, make a pencil mark by each thing as you count.

Count each group of insects. Write each number in the box.

A.  

B.  

C. 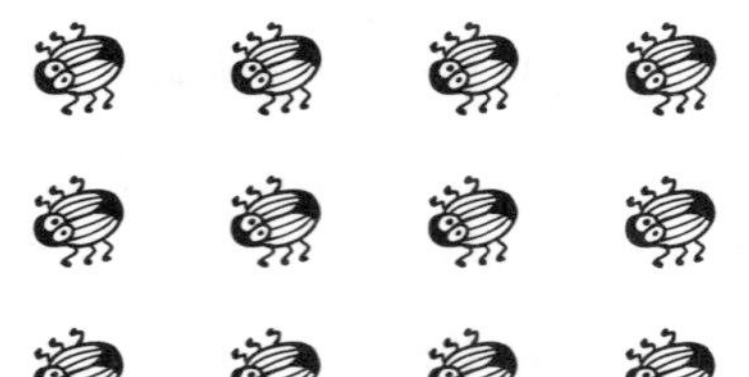

D. 

E. 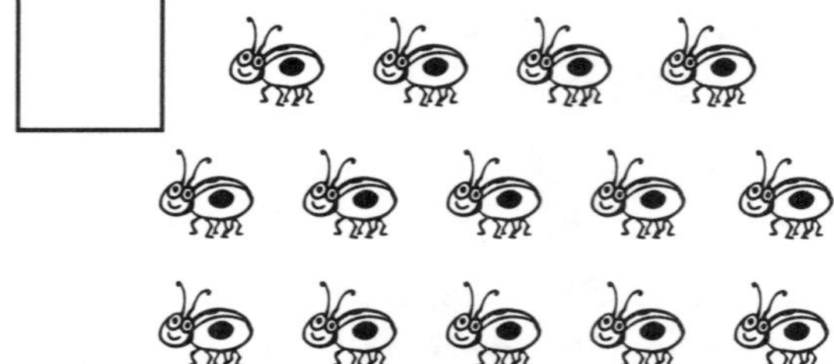

F. 

G. 

 Draw 8 bugs.

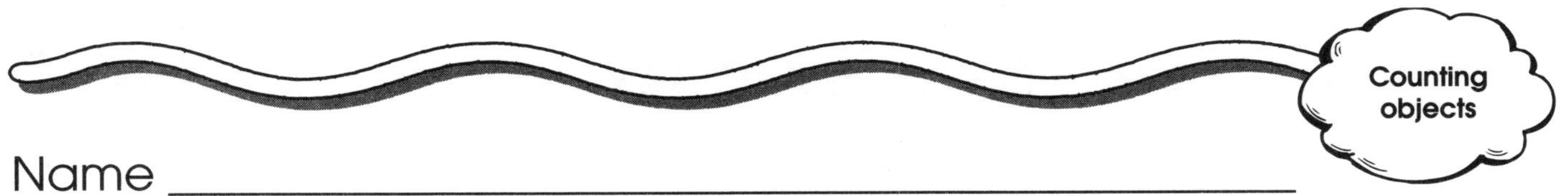

Name ______________________________

Camp Count

Count the number of each thing in the picture. Write the number on the line next to each thing below.

______ ______ ______

______ ______ ______

______ ______ ______

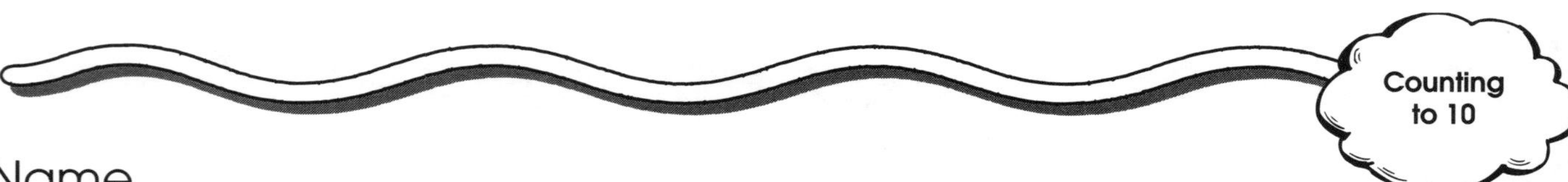

Name ______________________________

Roll That Number

Every number can be written as a word.   three

Count each group of balls. Draw a line from the balls to the correct number word.

five

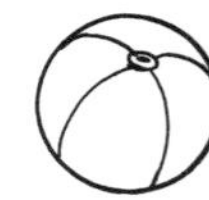  

nine

three

six

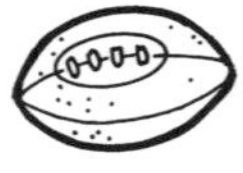

one

ten

four

eight

two

seven

Draw eleven balls.

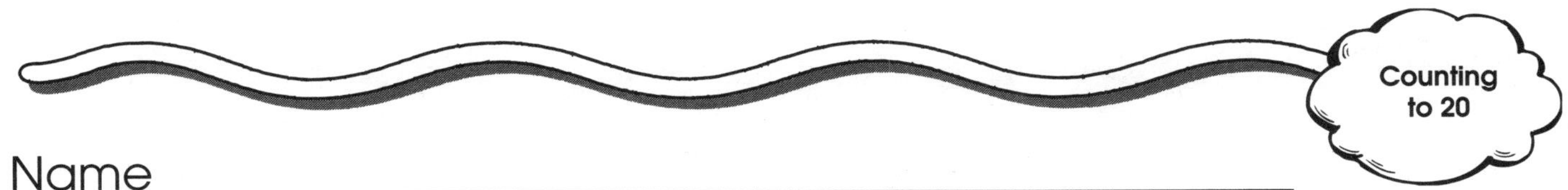

Name ______________________________

Dash to 20

Write the numbers in order from 1 to 20 on the shoes.

START

FINISH

Counting by ones

Name ______________________________

Travel to 30

Write the missing number in each box.

A. 4 5 ___

B.

13 ___ 15

C. ___ 23 24

D.

1 2 ___

E. 19 ___ 21

F. 10 ___ 12

G. 25 26 ___

H.

___ 8 9

I. ___ 29 30

J.

16 ___ 18

Cut out each box. Then, place the boxes in number order from 1 to 30.

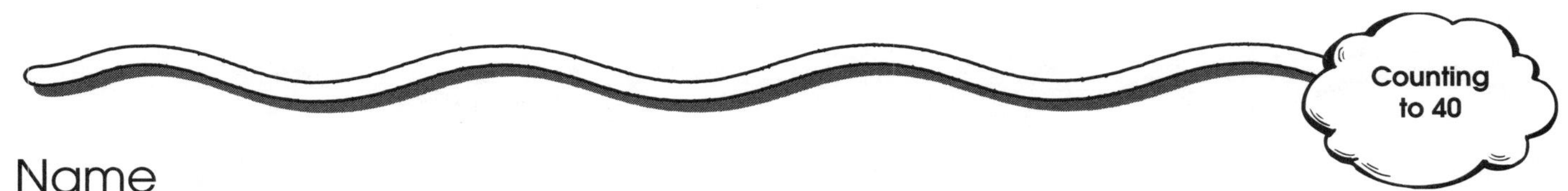

Name ______________________________

An "Arm"y of Numbers

Connect the dots from 1 to 40. Color the sea animal.

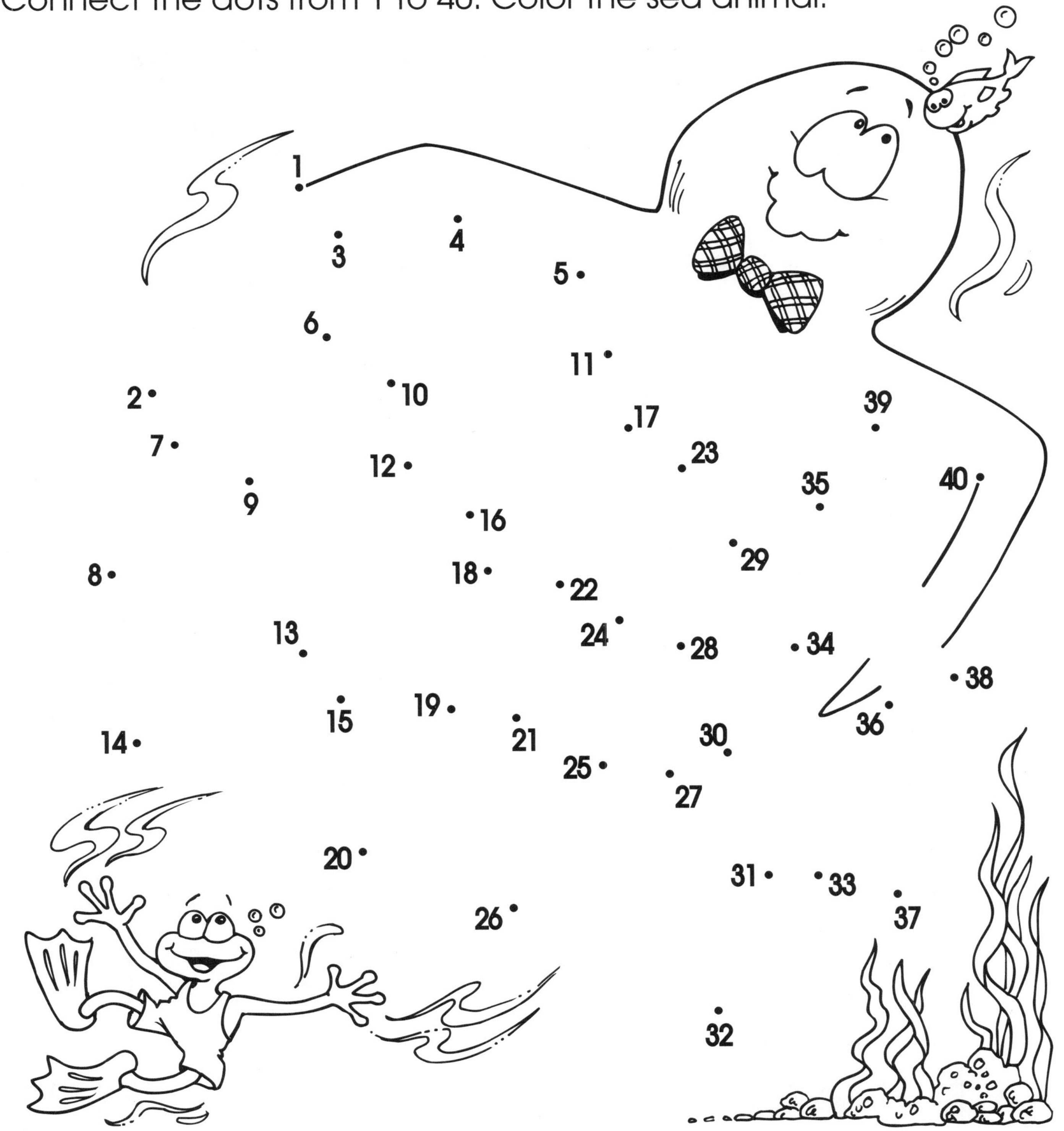

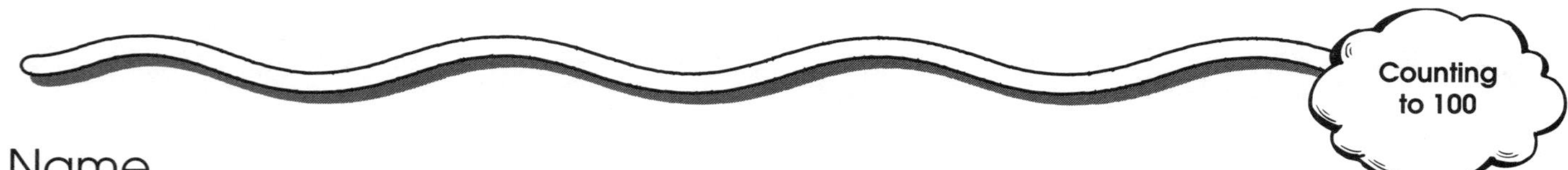

Name ______________________________

Let's Count

Use the chart to practice counting to 100.

Write each missing number.

1	2		4				8	9	
11					16				
				25		27	28		30
	32			35				39	
41		43			46	47			50
	52		54	55			58		
61			64			67	68		
		73		75				79	80
	82					87			
		93			96				100

Before, between, after

Name ______________________________

The Winning Number

The number 15 comes one before 16.
The number 35 comes between 34 and 36.
The number 49 comes one after 48.

Write the number that comes one before.

A.		5	B.		89
C.		23	D.		17

Write the number that comes between.

E.	11		13
F.	35		37
G.	62		64

Write the number that comes one after.

H.	79	
I.	50	
J.	41	

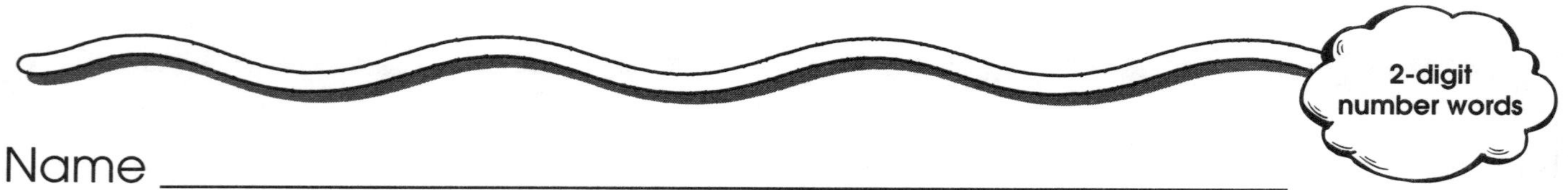

Name ____

Speedy Skaters

Which skater will win the race? To find out, color the space for each number as you read its name. The winner is the first skater to reach the snowman. Color the winning skater.

A. fifty-seven
B. nineteen
C. thirty-six
D. ninety-six
E. twenty
F. sixty-eight
G. eleven
H. eighty-two
I. seventy-four
J. thirty-one
K. fifty-four
L. seventy-nine
M. forty-three
N. twelve
O. twenty-five
P. forty-seven

57 19 96 11 54 79 12 47

FINISH

25 43 31 74 82 68 20 36

Name ______________________________

Flipping Forward

Counting by 2s or 5s is called **skip counting**.

A. Count the flippers by 2s. Write each number.

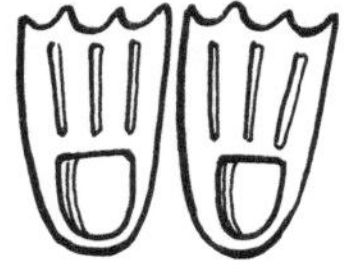 +  +  +  +

_____ _____ _____ _____ _____

\+ + + +

_____ _____ _____ _____ _____

B. Count the toes by 5s. Write each number.

\+ + + + +

_____ _____ _____ _____ _____ _____

\+ + + + +

_____ _____ _____ _____ _____ _____

Name ____

Skip to 100

A quick way to count to 100 is by 5s or 10s.

A. Count by 5s. Circle the numbers as you count.

B. Count by 10s. Color the numbers yellow as you count.

1	2	3	4	5	6	7	8	9	10
11	12	13	14	15	16	17	18	19	20
21	22	23	24	25	26	27	28	29	30
31	32	33	34	35	36	37	38	39	40
41	42	43	44	45	46	47	48	49	50
51	52	53	54	55	56	57	58	59	60
61	62	63	64	65	66	67	68	69	70
71	72	73	74	75	76	77	78	79	80
81	82	83	84	85	86	87	88	89	90
91	92	93	94	95	96	97	98	99	100

Name ______________________________

Blast off!

You have been practicing counting forward. Now let's practice counting back.

A. Write the number of stars on each rocket.

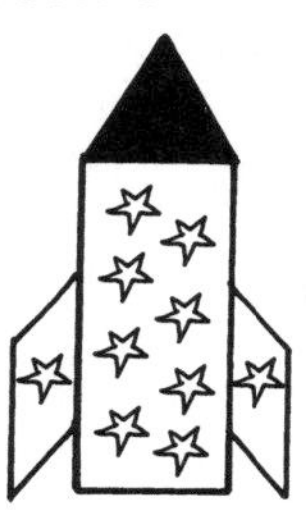 ______ 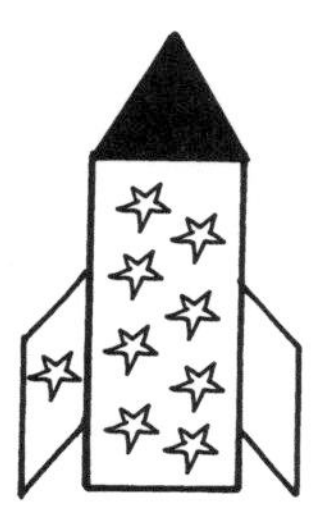 ______ 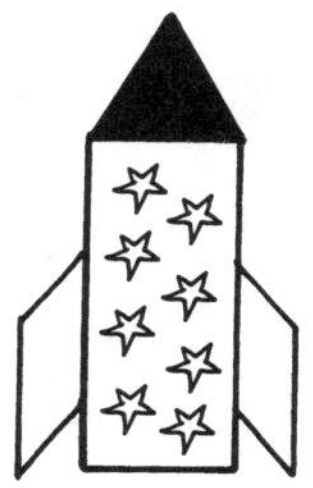 ______  ______  ______

 ______ 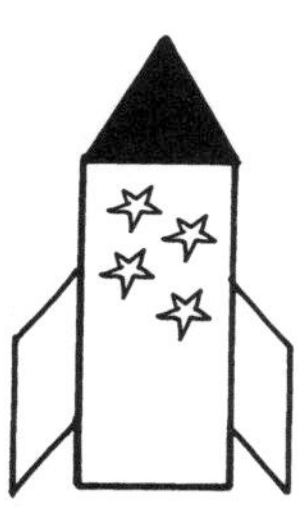 ______  ______ 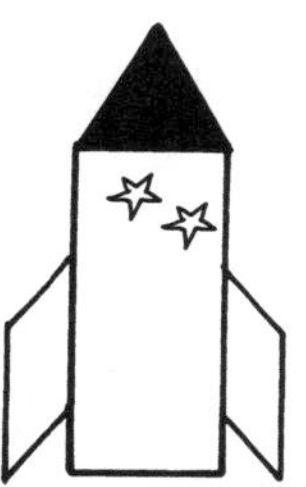 ______  ______

B. Count back. Write each missing number.

4, 3, ____, 1

8, ____, ____, 5

10, 9, ____, ____

____, ____, 4, 3

Name ______________________________

Note the Number

A. Write each missing number on the notebook.

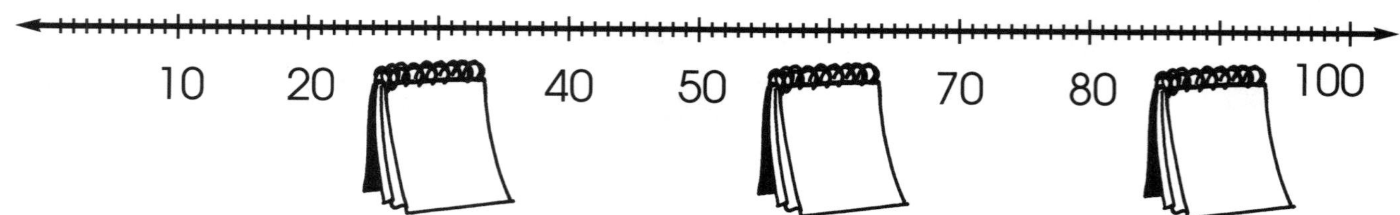

Count back by tens.

B. 100, 90, 80, _____, _____, _____, _____, _____, _____, 10

C. 50, _____, 30, 20, 10

D. 90, 80, _____, _____, 50

E. 70, _____, 50, _____, 30

F. _____, _____, 60, 50, _____

G. _____, 50, _____, _____

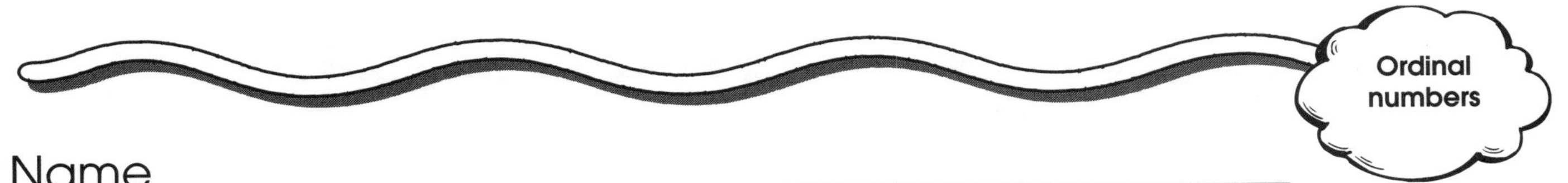

Name ______________________________

Dinnertime

Ordinal numbers show the position of things.

Follow the directions to show each animal's place in line.

Color the third animal brown.
Color the fifth animal gray.
Color the eighth animal red.
Color the first animal blue.
Color the sixth animal orange.
Color the tenth animal green.
Color the second animal pink.
Color the fourth animal yellow.
Color the seventh animal purple.
Color the ninth animal white.

Even and odd numbers

Name ____

Candle Count

Even numbers end in 0, 2, 4, 6, and 8.
Odd numbers end in 1, 3, 5, 7, and 9.

Count the candles on each cake. Write the number on the cake. Color each cake with an even number.

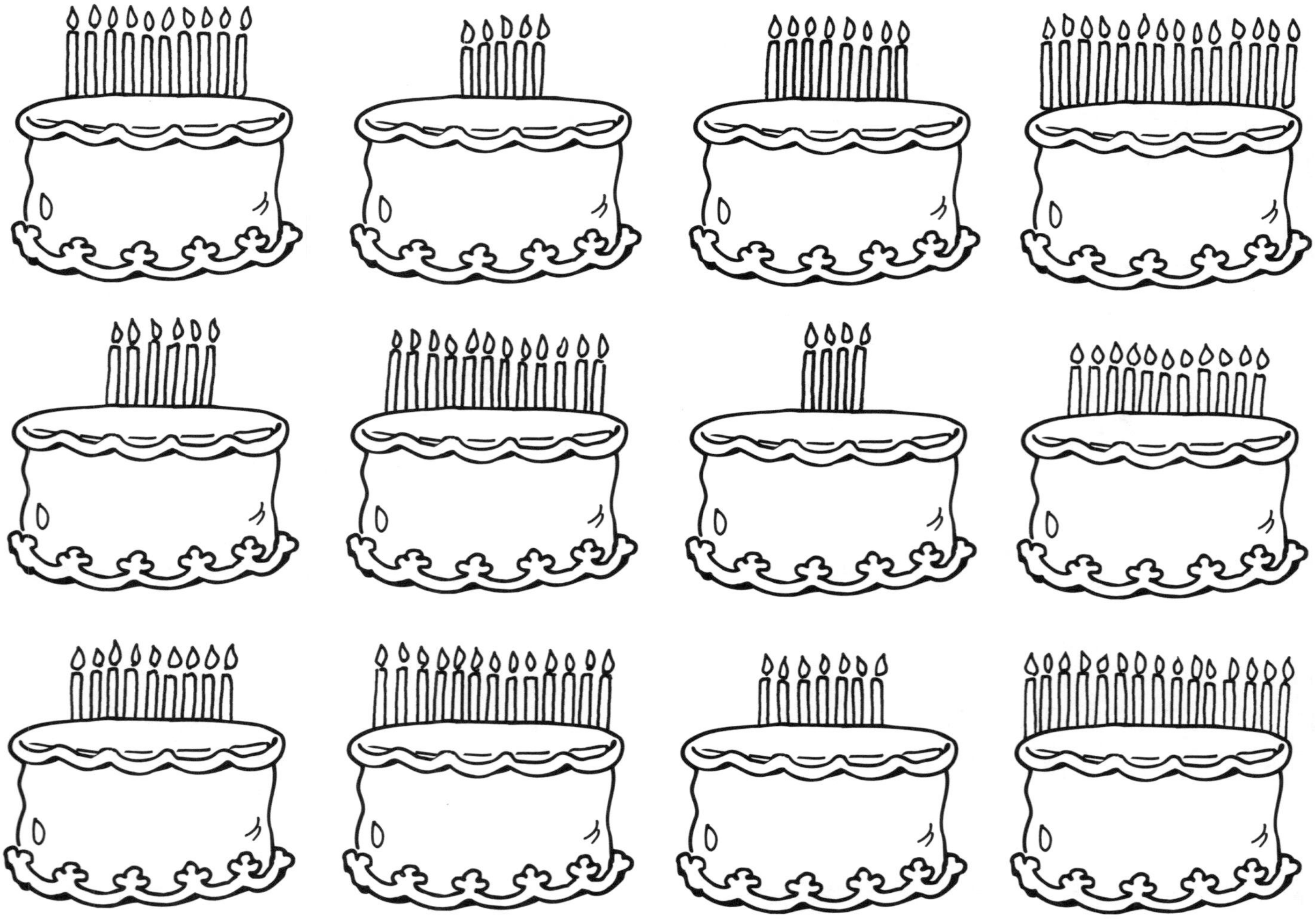

Draw candles on the cake to show how old you are.

Is your age even or odd? ____________

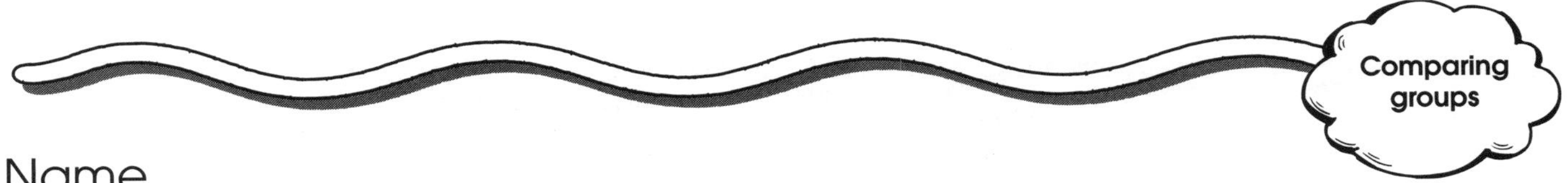

Name ______________________________

Sweet Treats

There are **more** .

There are **fewer** .

Count how many. Write the number. Circle each group with more.

A. ☐ ☐

B. ☐ ☐

C. ☐ ☐

D. ☐ ☐

E. ☐ ☐

F. ☐ ☐

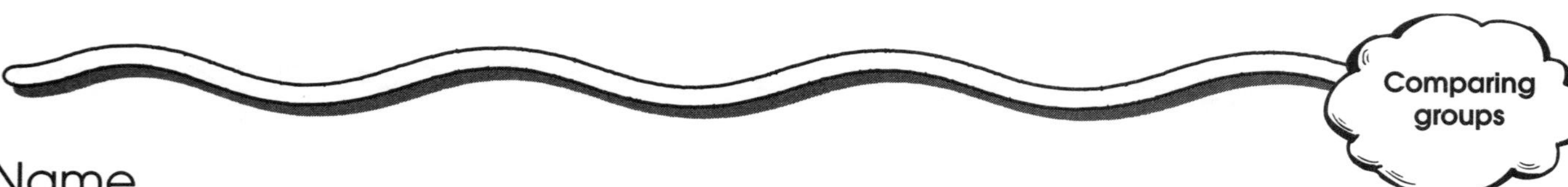

Name ______________________________

Cat Nap

Fewer means the amount with less.

Circle each basket with fewer cats.

A.

B.

C.

D.

E.

F.

G.

Draw fewer cats in the empty basket.

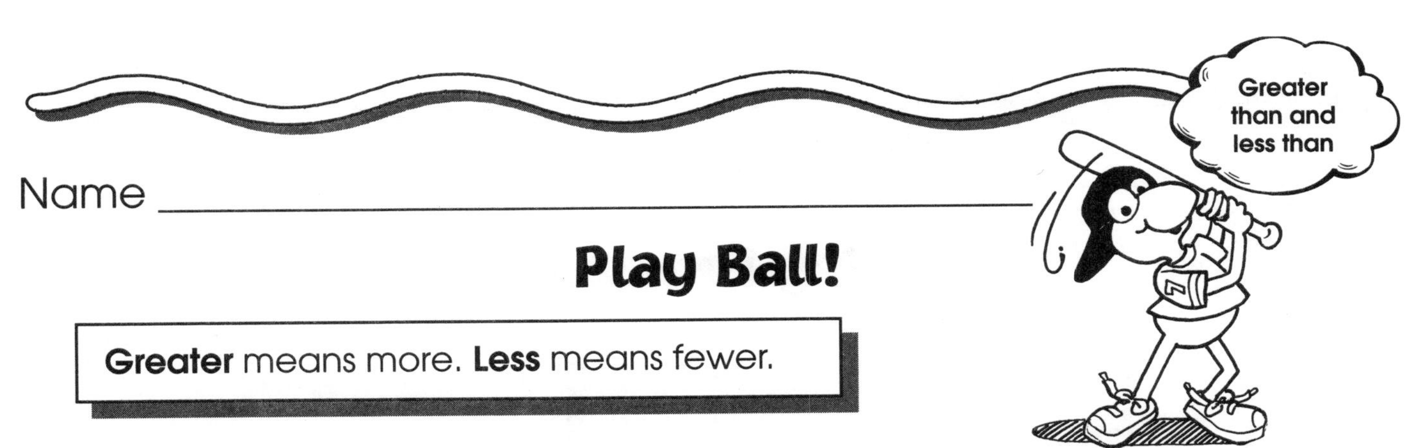

Name ______________________________

Play Ball!

Greater means more. **Less** means fewer.

Circle the group of balls in each box with the greater number.

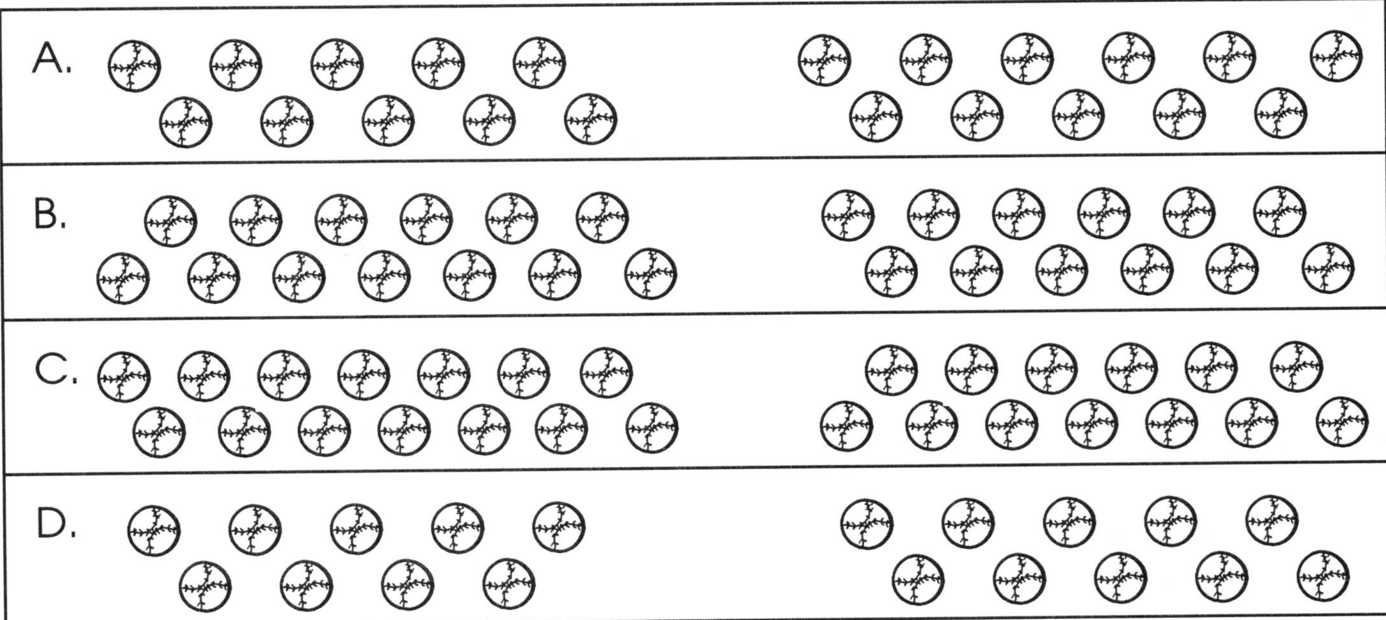

A.

B.

C.

D.

Circle the group of bats in each box with the least number.

E.

F.

G.

H.

Name ______________________________

Fry Frenzy

(4 fries) is **greater than** (2 fries).		4 > 2
(1 fry) is **less than** (3 fries).		1 < 3

Compare the number of French fries in the bags. Write **>** or **<** in the circle between them.

A. 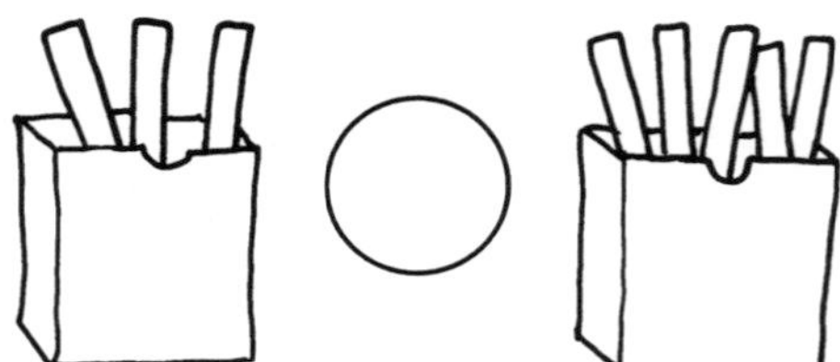

B. 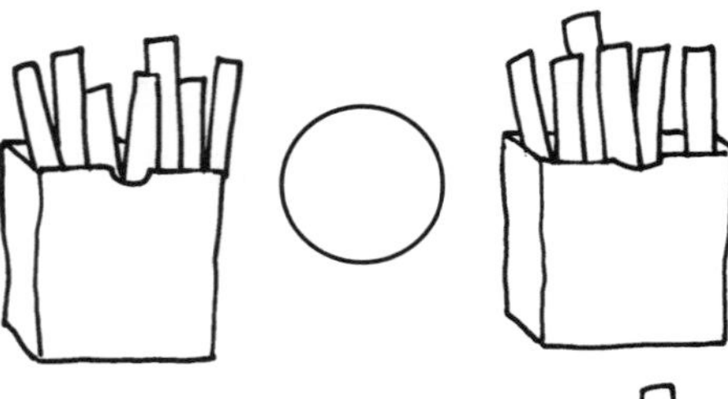

C. 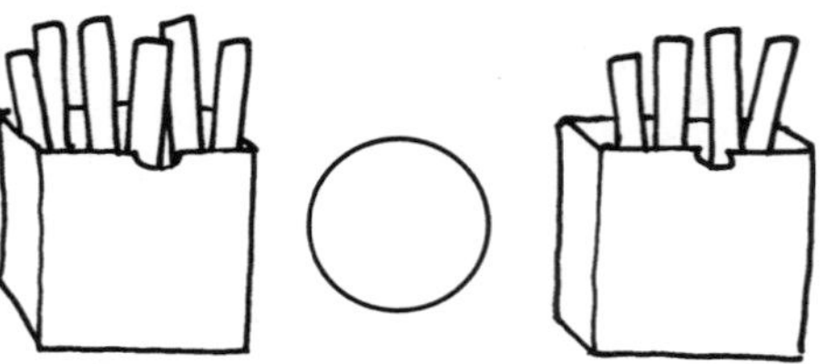

D. 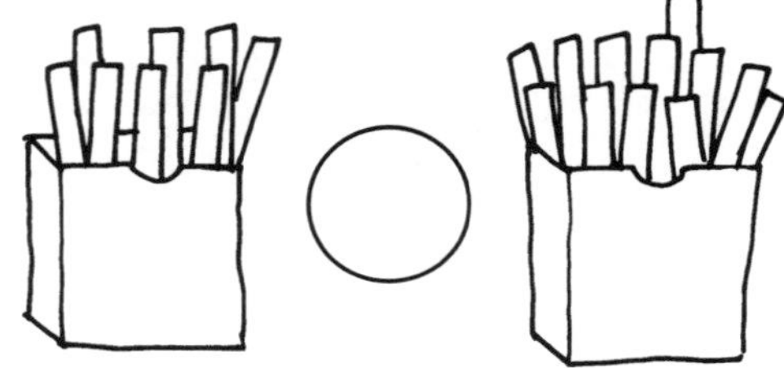

E. 

F. 

G. 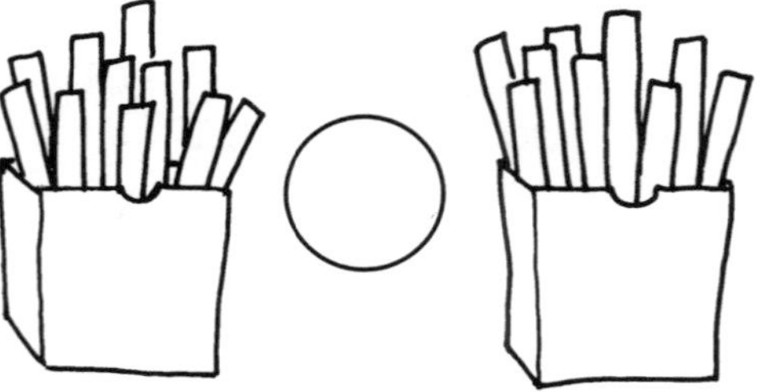

H. 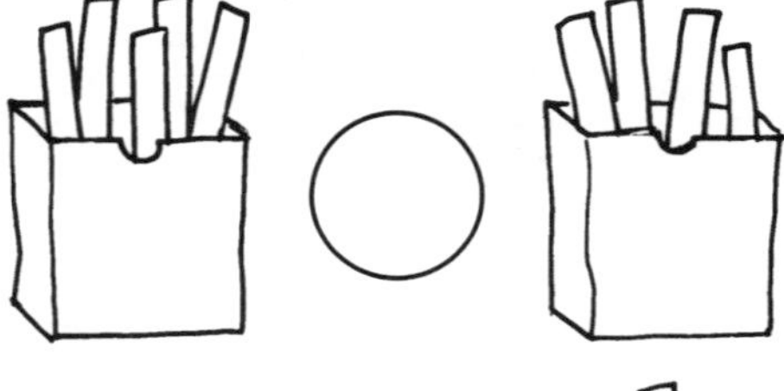

I. 

J. 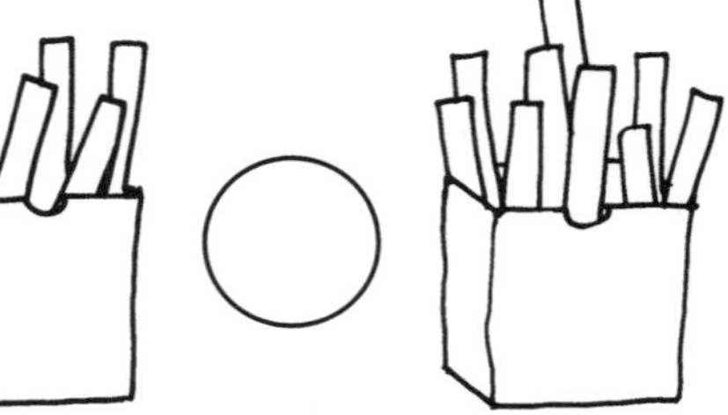

Greater than and less than

Name ______________________________

Open Wide

Remember, the sign is open to the greater number.
The sign > means **greater than**. The sign < means **less than**.

Write > or < in the circle between each set of numbers.

A. 15 ◯ 12

B. 8 ◯ 14

C. 6 ◯ 8

D. 12 ◯ 21

E. 24 ◯ 17

F. 11 ◯ 9

G. 30 ◯ 29

H. 18 ◯ 22

I. 10 ◯ 13

J. 20 ◯ 15

K. 19 ◯ 16

L. 3 ◯ 4

Name ____

Mail Order

Write the numbers in order from least to greatest on the mailboxes.

A. 53 27 19

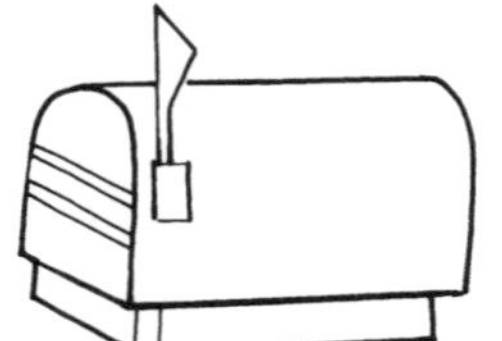 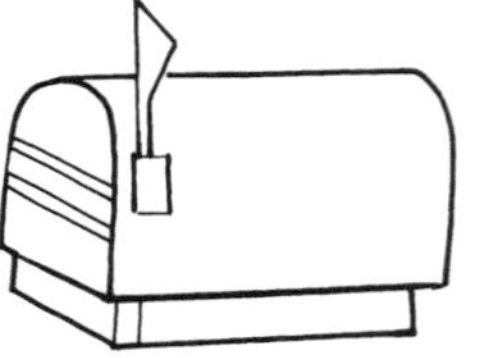 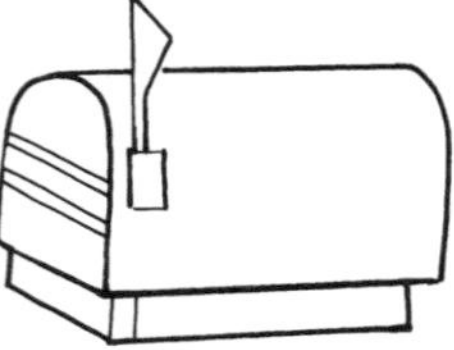

B. 48 31 64

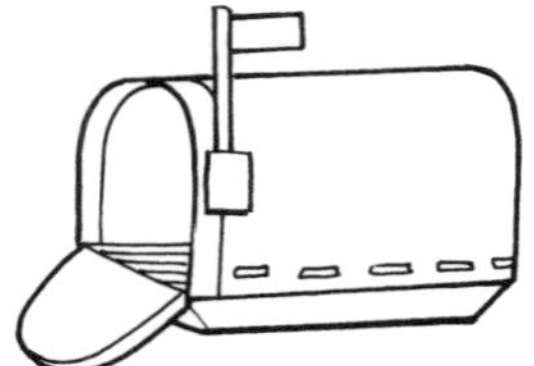 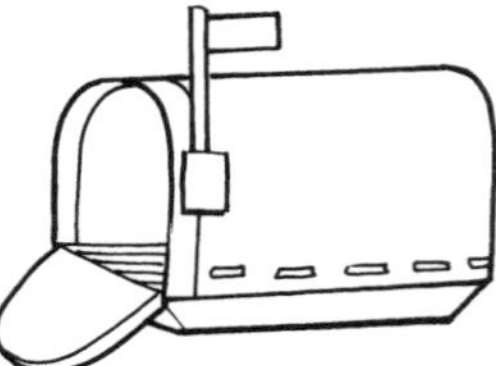 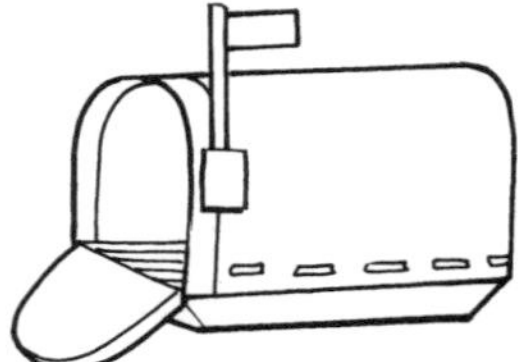

C. 12 36 25

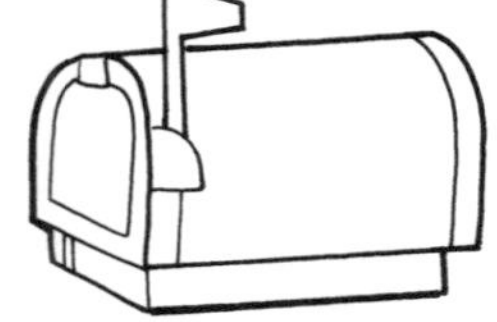 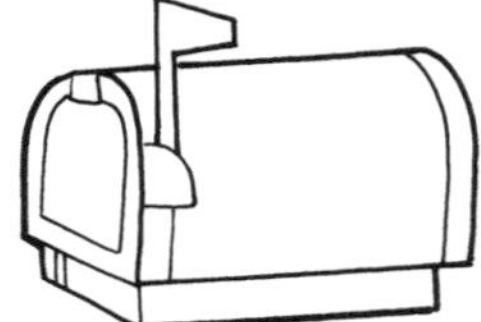 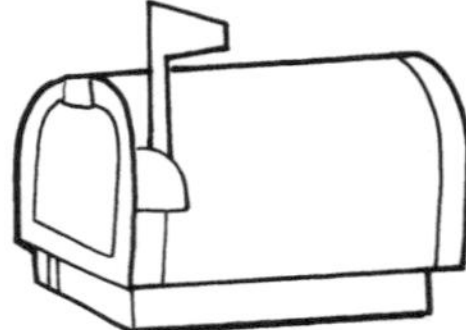

D. 83 74 67

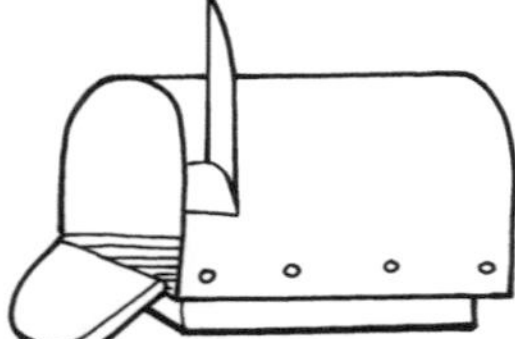 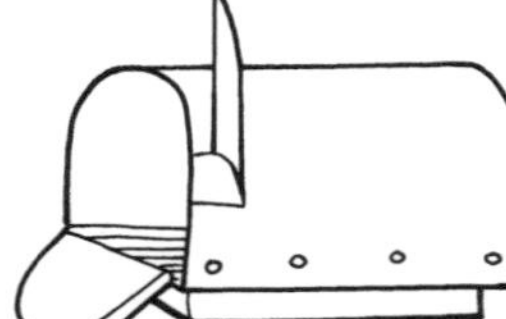 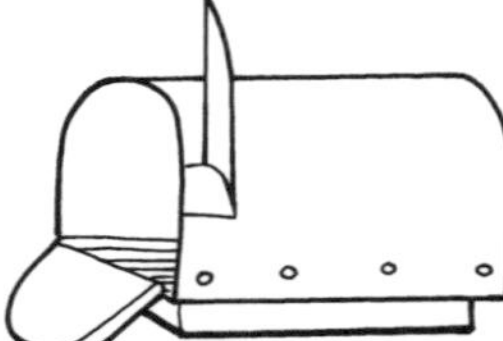

E. 61 54 92

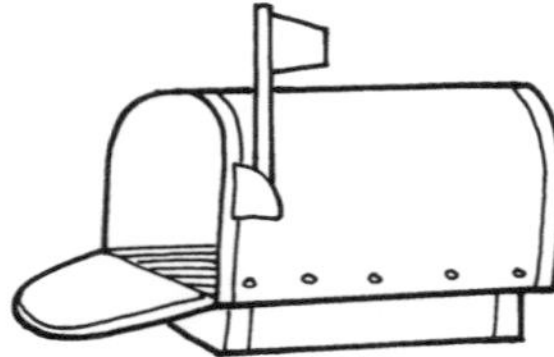 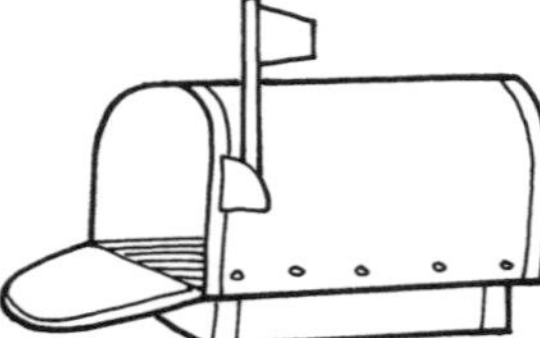 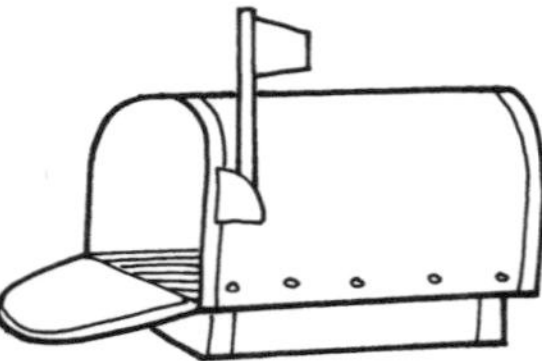

Write four numbers greater than 20 on the mailboxes in order from least to greatest.

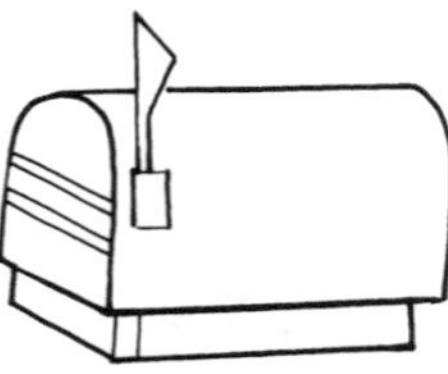 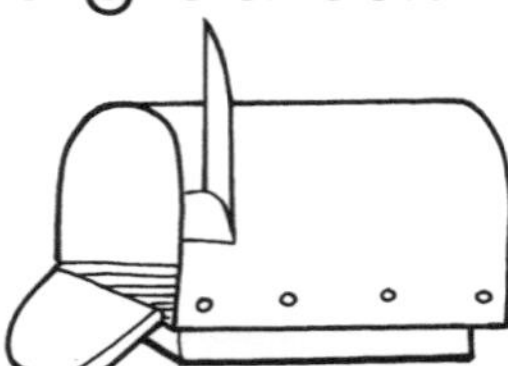 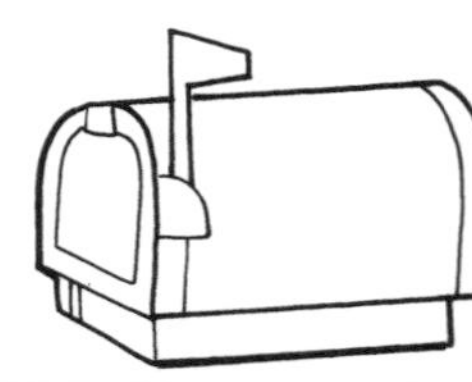 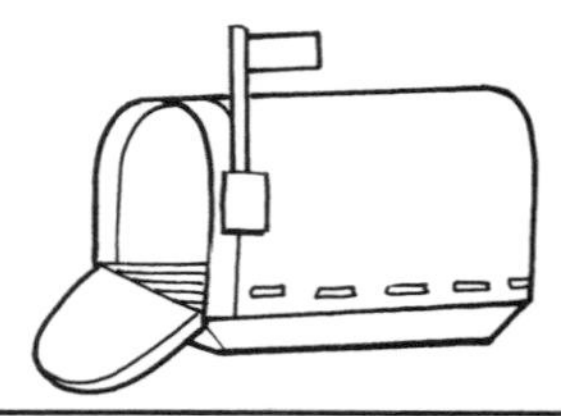

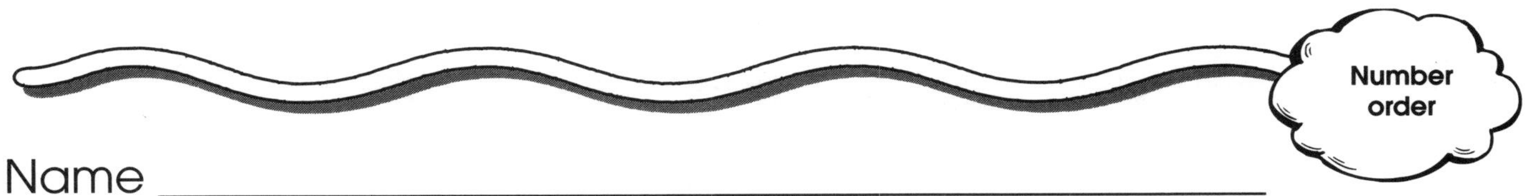

Name ______________________________

Scoop the Number

Write each number from the bucket on the correct sand castle.

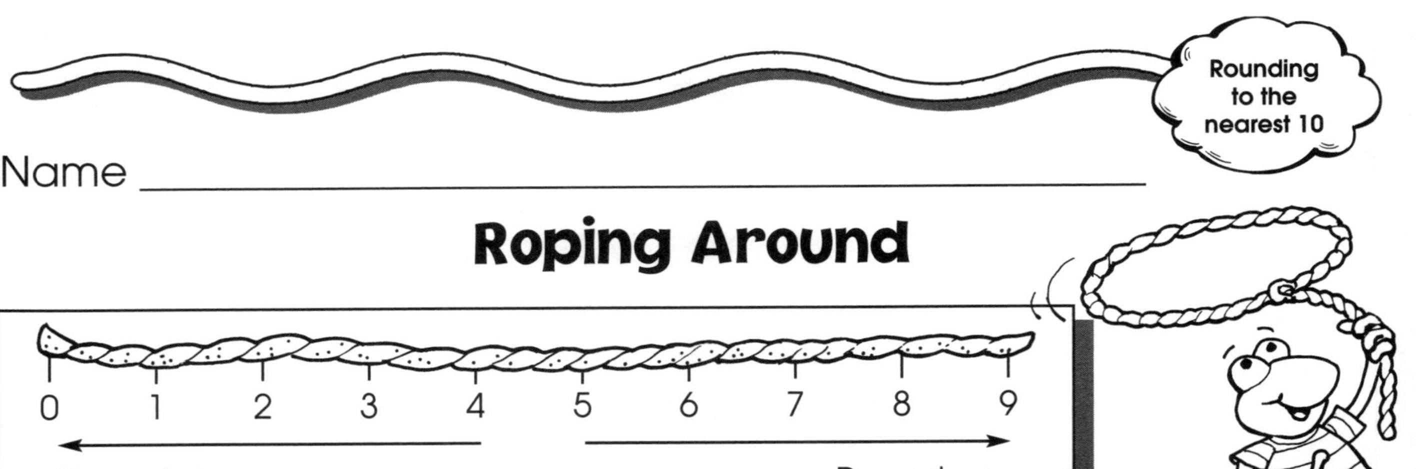

Name ______________________________

Roping Around

Look at the ones digit. Then, round each number to the nearest 10.

A. 62 ☐ 39 ☐ 27 ☐

B. 45 ☐ 71 ☐ 14 ☐

C. 86 ☐ 53 ☐ 78 ☐

D. 24 ☐ 41 ☐ 65 ☐

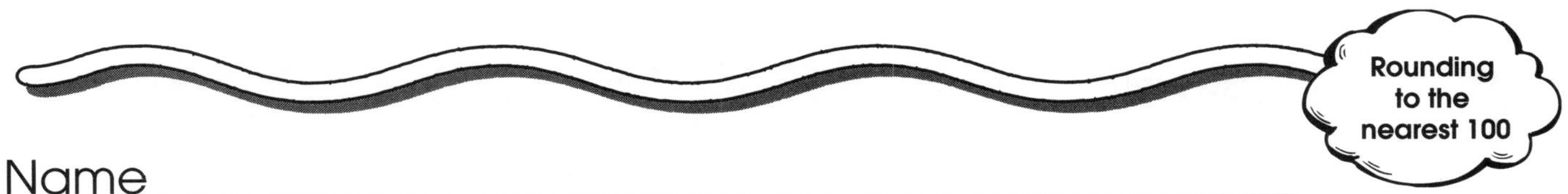

Name ______________________________

Coin Count

When rounding to the nearest hundred, look at the number in the tens place.

Round the number of pennies in each bank to the nearest hundred. Color the banks you rounded up to show the path to the bank.

153 849 621 407

394 672 238 716 425

583 169 357 909 734

816 422 263 685

Bank

Name ______________________________

Sum Fun

The answer to an addition problem is the **sum**.

Use the pictures to help you find each sum.

A.  

3 + 2 = _____

B.  

6 + 3 = _____

C.  

4 + 2 = _____

D.  

1 + 9 = _____

E.  

1 + 3 = _____

F.  

5 + 4 = _____

G.   

4 + 4 = _____

 Write the number sentence for the pictures.

_____ + _____ = _____

Sums 12 and less

Name ______________________________

Fruity Facts

Use the pictures to help you find each sum.

A.

7 + 5 = ______

B.

9 + 2 = ______

C.

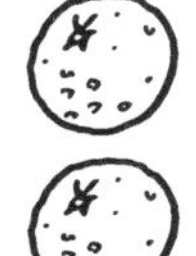

2 + 8 = ______

D.

5 + 5 = ______

E.

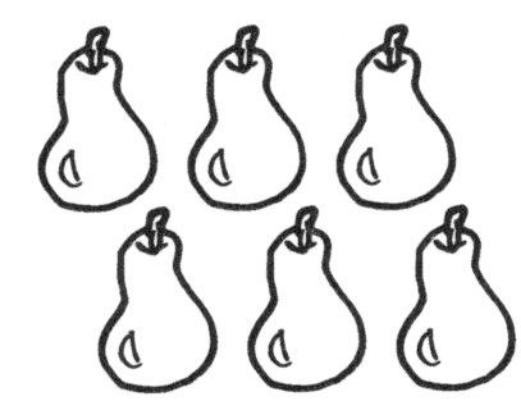

6 + 6 = ______

F.

3 + 9 = ______

G.

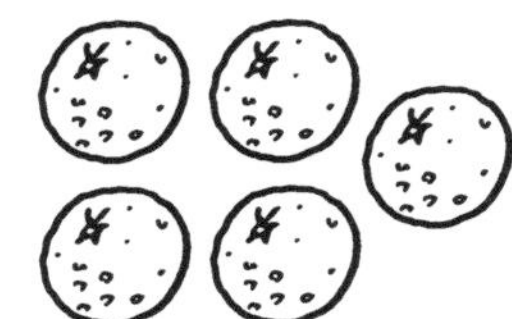

4 + 7 = ______

H.

5 + 6 = ______

Name ______________________________

Inch by Inch

You can use a number line to help you add.

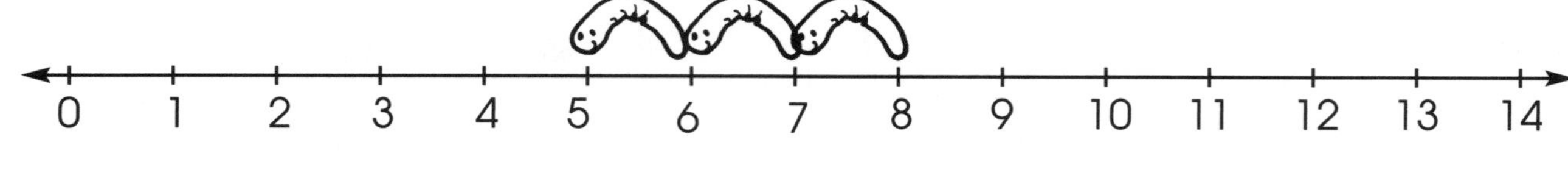

5 + 3 = ____ Start at 5. Count on 3 more—6, 7, 8. 5 + 3 = 8

Use the number line to help you add.

A. 4 + 6 = ______

B. 6 + 8 = ______

C. 8 + 4 = ______

D. 5 + 5 = ______

E. 7 + 7 = ______

F. 9 + 3 = ______

G. 5 + 4 = ______

H. 7 + 6 = ______

I. 3 + 8 = ______

J. 2 + 6 = ______

K. 5 + 9 = ______

L. 8 + 3 = ______

M. 0 + 9 = ______

N. 5 + 6 = ______

O. 6 + 1 = ______

P. 4 + 7 = ______

Sums 14 and less

Name ____________________

Let It Snow!

6 + 3 = 9 can also be written

$$\begin{array}{r} 6 \\ +\ 3 \\ \hline 9 \end{array}$$

Use the pictures to help you add.

A. $\begin{array}{r} 4 \\ +\ 6 \\ \hline \end{array}$ $\begin{array}{r} 5 \\ +\ 7 \\ \hline \end{array}$ $\begin{array}{r} 2 \\ +\ 9 \\ \hline \end{array}$

B. $\begin{array}{r} 3 \\ +\ 7 \\ \hline \end{array}$ $\begin{array}{r} 6 \\ +\ 8 \\ \hline \end{array}$ $\begin{array}{r} 9 \\ +\ 4 \\ \hline \end{array}$

Add.

C. $\begin{array}{r} 6 \\ +\ 5 \\ \hline \end{array}$ $\begin{array}{r} 2 \\ +\ 7 \\ \hline \end{array}$ $\begin{array}{r} 5 \\ +\ 8 \\ \hline \end{array}$

D. $\begin{array}{r} 7 \\ +\ 7 \\ \hline \end{array}$ $\begin{array}{r} 5 \\ +\ 9 \\ \hline \end{array}$ $\begin{array}{r} 4 \\ +\ 3 \\ \hline \end{array}$

E. $\begin{array}{r} 8 \\ +\ 4 \\ \hline \end{array}$ $\begin{array}{r} 9 \\ +\ 0 \\ \hline \end{array}$ $\begin{array}{r} 7 \\ +\ 6 \\ \hline \end{array}$

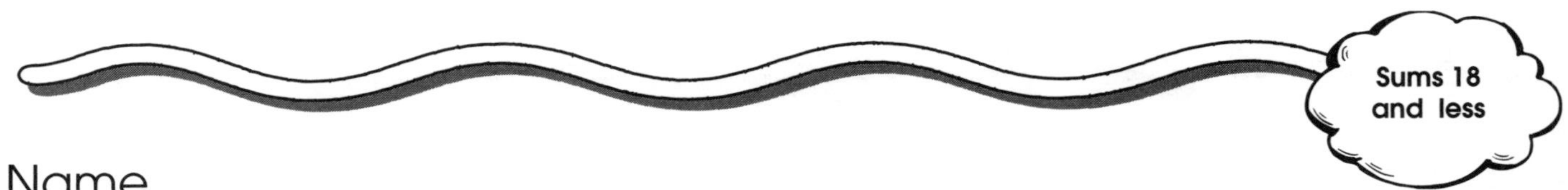

Name ______________________________

Race Ahead

Add. Then, color each square with a sum equal to 10 to race the car to the flag.

	5 + 5	4 + 3	8 + 7	2 + 6
7 + 7	3 + 7	9 + 1	9 + 8	4 + 5
8 + 8	5 + 3	6 + 4	9 + 9	2 + 7
5 + 6	7 + 3	2 + 8	3 + 8	7 + 9
7 + 8	1 + 9	6 + 9	7 + 4	
9 + 6	4 + 6	8 + 2	5 + 5	

Name ____________________

Space Math

Add. Then, use the code to answer the riddle.

What is soft and white and comes from Mars?

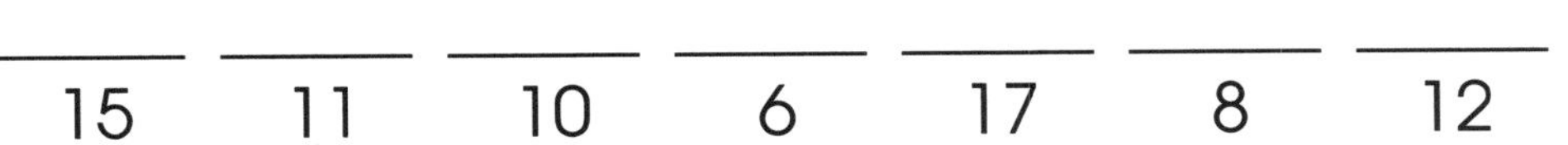

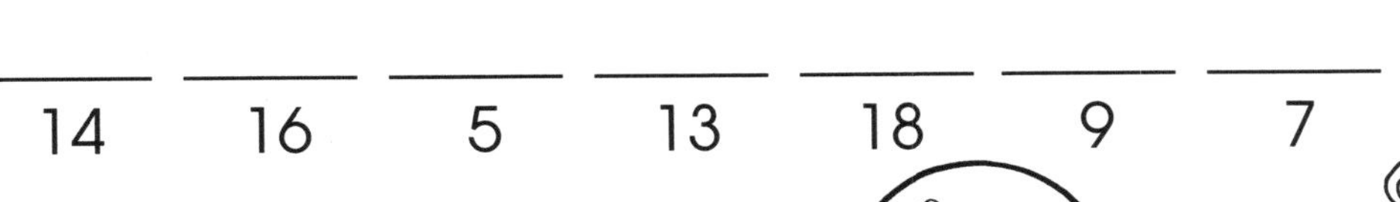

5 + 6 = ___ **A**	8 + 9 = ___ **I**				
8 + 8 = ___ **A**	3 + 4 = ___ **S**	2 + 8 = ___ **R**	6 + 8 = ___ **M**	9 + 6 = ___ **M**	1 + 5 = ___ **T**
7 + 5 = ___ **N**	3 + 5 = ___ **A**	7 + 6 = ___ **L**	2 + 7 = ___ **W**	9 + 9 = ___ **O**	2 + 3 = ___ **L**

Sums 18 and less

Name ______________________________

Addition Magician

Add.

A. 4 + 6 = ___ 8 + 6 = ___ 4 + 4 = ___ 3 + 1 = ___ 5 + 2 = ___

B. 9 + 3 = ___ 6 + 5 = ___ 7 + 8 = ___ 2 + 4 = ___ 5 + 9 = ___

C. 8 + 9 = ___ 2 + 2 = ___ 6 + 1 = ___ 3 + 7 = ___ 0 + 5 = ___

D. 4 + 5 = ___ 8 + 2 = ___ 7 + 6 = ___ 9 + 9 = ___ 1 + 4 = ___

E. 9 + 6 = ___ 5 + 6 = ___ 8 + 8 = ___

On another piece of paper, write five addition problems with a sum of 12.

Missing addends

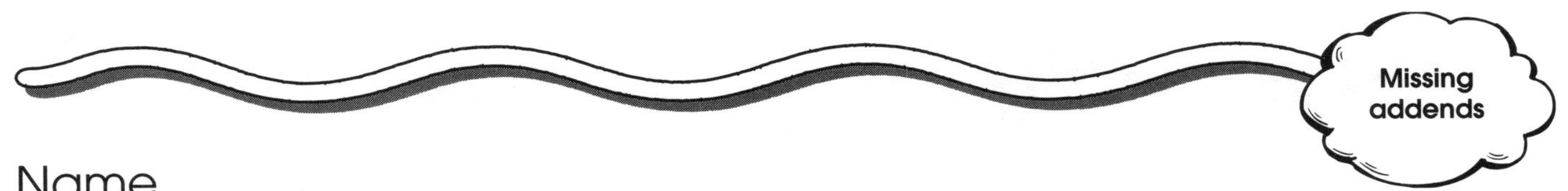

Name ____

Don't Miss!

Write the missing number in each number sentence. Then, color each basketball with the missing number of 5 to follow the path to the player who made the winning basket.

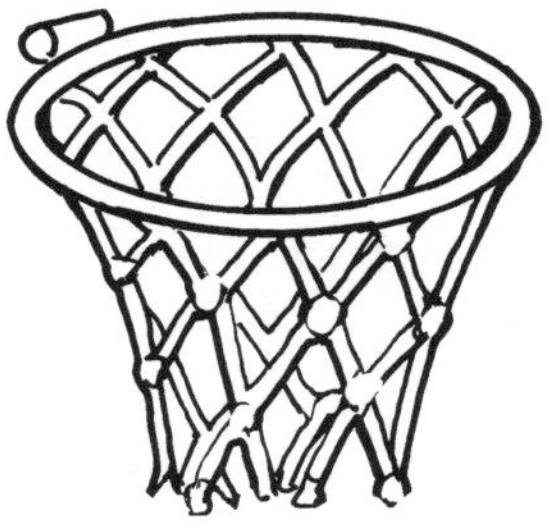

	5 + ___ = 10	___ + 2 = 10	8 + ___ = 12	9 + ___ = 18
___ + 6 = 12	___ + 6 = 11	1 + ___ = 7	___ + 3 = 6	4 + ___ = 11
7 + ___ = 14	___ + 4 = 9	___ + 2 = 7	___ + 4 = 6	9 + ___ = 17
	6 + ___ = 12	3 + ___ = 8	5 + ___ = 13	
	9 + ___ = 15	___ + 1 = 6	9 + ___ = 14	

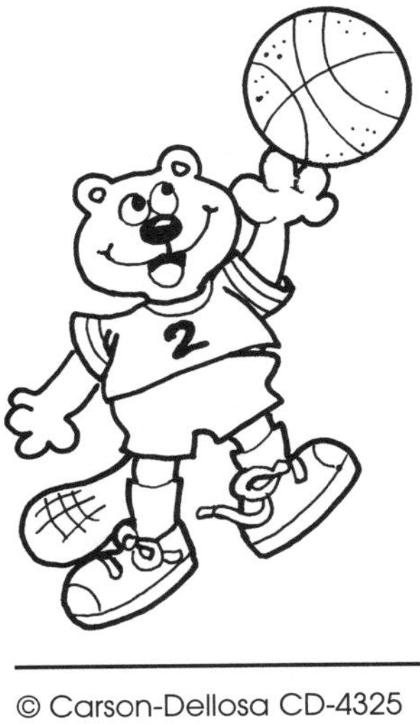

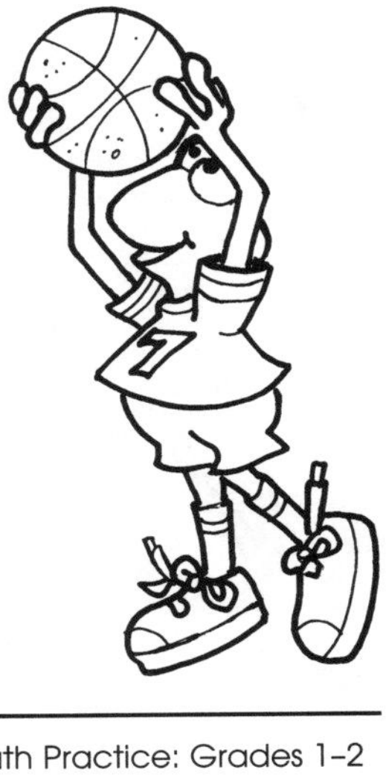

Name ______________________________

Find the Fact

When finding the sum of three addends, look for a fact you know.

6 + 2 = 8, then + 4	2 + 4 = 6, then + 6	6 + 4 = 10, then + 2
$8 + 4 = 12$	$6 + 6 = 12$	$10 + 2 = 12$

Circle the numbers you would add first. Add.

A.

3	2	7	6
5	8	1	4
+ 4	+ 6	+ 5	+ 1

B.

9	4	2	3
2	5	1	3
+ 3	+ 4	+ 6	+ 5

C.

2	8	1	5
1	2	7	6
+ 9	+ 7	+ 3	+ 2

Name ____

The Key to the Story

The key words "in all" and "altogether" in a word problem tell you to add.

Circle the key words in each story. Finish each number sentence to solve the problem.

A. Sam has 5 cookies. Jake has 4 cookies. How many cookies do the boys have altogether?

_____ + _____ = _____ cookies

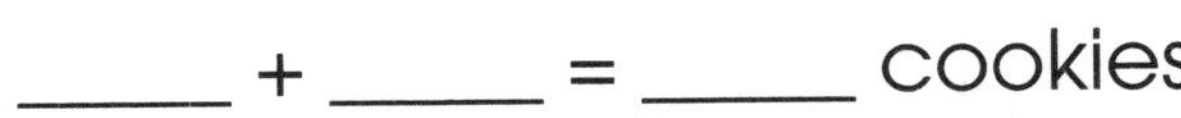

B. Lisa has 3 pencils in her box. She has 8 pencils on her desk. How many pencils does Lisa have altogether?

_____ + _____ = _____ pencils

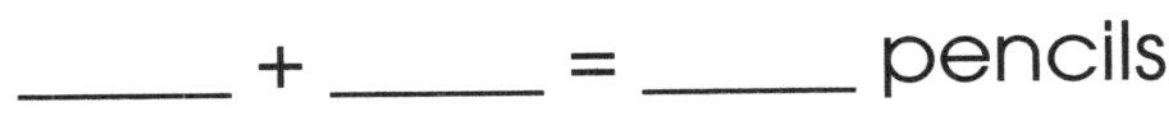

C. There are 2 puppies sleeping. Then, 5 more puppies fall asleep. How many puppies are sleeping in all?

_____ + _____ = _____ puppies

D. Annie counted 6 stars on Monday. She counted 7 stars on Tuesday. How many stars did Annie count in all?

_____ + _____ = _____ stars

Name ______________________________

Game Time

> Always write the unit in the answer of a word problem.
>
> I played 3 games yesterday. Today I played 2 games. How many games did I play altogether?
>
> 3 + 2 = 5 games

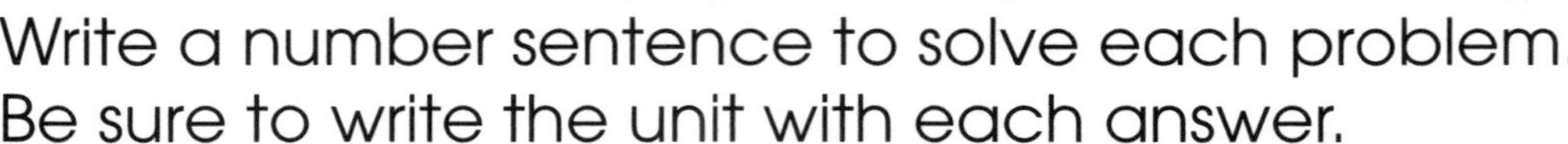

Write a number sentence to solve each problem. Be sure to write the unit with each answer.

A. Tyler hit 8 balls over the fence. Jack hit 6 balls over the fence. How many balls in all were hit over the fence?	B. There are 6 games in Tara's room. There are 4 games in Jane's room. How many games do the girls have in all?
C. Connor has 9 marbles in his bag. He finds 5 more marbles. How many marbles does Connor have altogether?	D. Susan ran 3 laps around the track. Alex ran 9 laps around the track. How many laps did they run in all?
E. Kristen scored 7 goals. Kate scored 4 goals. How many goals did the girls score altogether?	F. In the first race, Nick swam for 8 minutes. In the next race, he swam for 5 minutes. How many minutes did Nick swim altogether?

Subtracting from 10 and less

Name ____________________

Who Ate the Cookies?

Subtracting means to take away from a group.
I have 3 cookies.
I ate 2 cookies.
I have 1 cookie left.

To help you subtract, cross out cookies in each jar. Then, subtract.

A.

4 – 1 = ______

B.

5 – 3 = ______

C.

2 – 2 = ______

D.

6 – 4 = ______

E.

3 – 1 = ______

F.

4 – 2 = ______

G.

6 – 3 = ______

H.

5 – 2 = ______

Subtracting from 10 and less

Name ______________________________

Check Your Pack

The answer to a subtraction problem is called the **difference**.

To help you subtract, cross out items in each backpack. Then, subtract.

A.

9 – 5 = ______

8 – 3 = ______

10 – 4 = ______

7 – 2 = ______

B.

10 – 7 = ______

6 – 2 = ______

4 – 3 = ______

9 – 3 = ______

C.

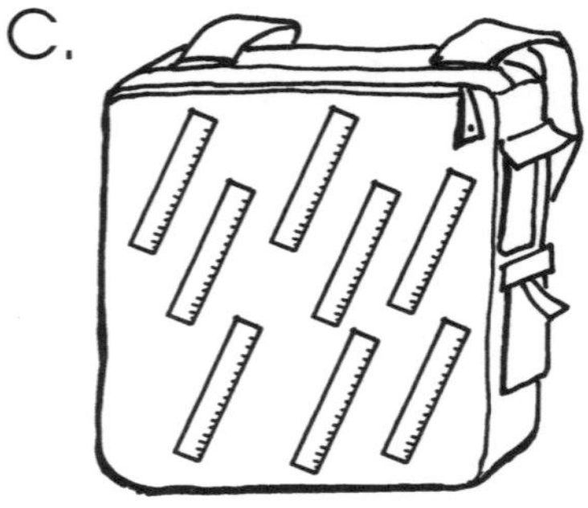

8 – 6 = ______

7 – 4 = ______

10 – 5 = ______

5 – 5 = ______

Subtracting from 14 and less

Name ______________________________

Flowering Facts

Subtract.

A.

11 − 5 = _____ 9 − 3 = _____ 13 − 4 = _____

B.

14 − 5 = _____ 12 − 6 = _____ 8 − 2 = _____

C.

10 − 4 = _____ 13 − 9 = _____ 7 − 5 = _____ 8 − 1 = _____

D.

12 − 3 = _____ 5 − 4 = _____ 14 − 7 = _____ 11 − 2 = _____

E.

13 − 6 = _____ 8 − 5 = _____ 10 − 5 = _____ 12 − 7 = _____

Fritz picked 6 flowers from the garden. How many flowers were left?

Writing subtraction problems

Name ______________________________

String It Up

9 – 3 = 6

Write a subtraction problem to match each picture. Subtract.

A.

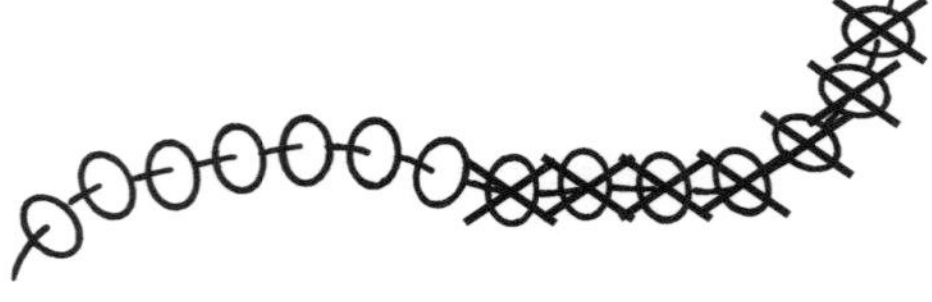

_____ – _____ = _____ _____ – _____ = _____ _____ – _____ = _____

B.

_____ – _____ = _____ _____ – _____ = _____ _____ – _____ = _____

C.

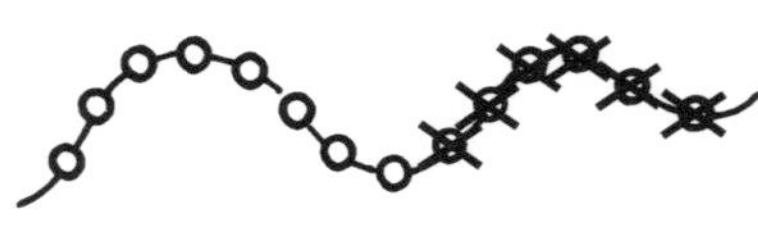

_____ – _____ = _____ _____ – _____ = _____ _____ – _____ = _____

On another piece of paper, draw your own string subtraction problem. Subtract.

Name ______________________________

Splish! Splash!

Subtract each row of problems in order. Cross off each difference on the slides as you subtract to see who splashes into the water first. Then, color the winning animal.

A. $12 - 8$ | $10 - 4$ | $8 - 3$ | $17 - 9$ | $5 - 5$ | $11 - 4$ | $18 - 9$ | $9 - 8$

12	10	8	17	5	11	18	9
− 8	− 4	− 3	− 9	− 5	− 4	− 9	− 8

B.

7	12	16	17	15	11	15	13
− 5	− 9	− 8	− 8	− 9	− 6	− 8	− 9

Name ______________________________

Break the Code

Use the code to write each subtraction problem. Then, subtract.

1 
2
3
4
5
6
7
8
9
10
11
12
13
14
15
16
17
18

A. 

_____ – _____ = _____

B. 

_____ – _____ = _____

C. 

_____ – _____ = _____

D.

_____ – _____ = _____

E. 

_____ – _____ = _____

F. 

_____ – _____ = _____

G. 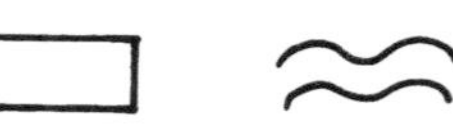

_____ – _____ = _____

H. 

_____ – _____ = _____

I. 

_____ – _____ = _____

J. 

_____ – _____ = _____

On another piece of paper, write three subtraction problems using the code.

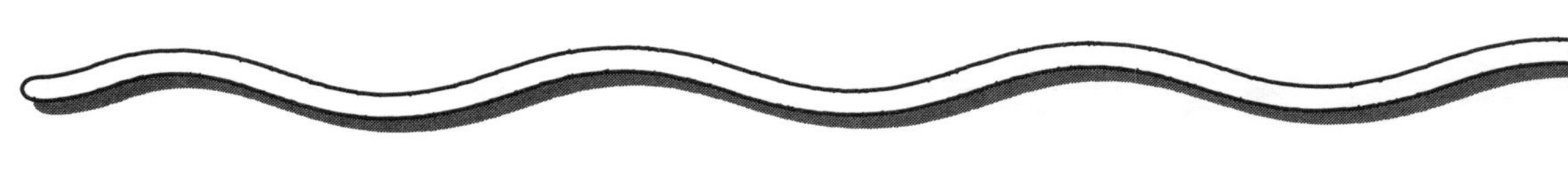

Subtracting from 18 and less

Name ______________________________

Subtraction Action

Subtract.

A.	15 − 7	10 − 7	6 − 5	18 − 9	12 − 6	8 − 4	14 − 5	5 − 2
B.	4 − 2	8 − 8	11 − 4	16 − 7	13 − 5	7 − 3	17 − 9	2 − 1
C.	5 − 1	9 − 6	14 − 7	17 − 8	7 − 5	16 − 8	9 − 4	11 − 6
D.	12 − 7	15 − 9			3 − 2	10 − 6	6 − 4	13 − 7

Name ______________________________

Family Picture

Fact families use the same numbers in addition and subtraction facts.

Complete each fact family.

A.

5 + 6 = _____

6 + 5 = _____

11 – 5 = _____

11 – 6 = _____

B.

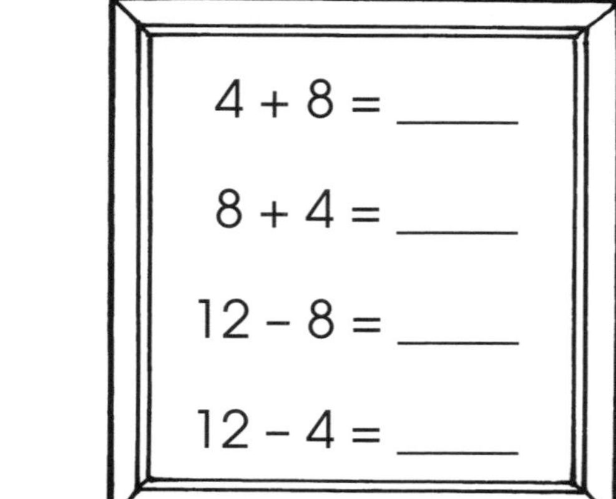

4 + 8 = _____

8 + 4 = _____

12 – 8 = _____

12 – 4 = _____

C.

7 + 8 = _____

8 + 7 = _____

15 – 7 = _____

15 – 8 = _____

D.

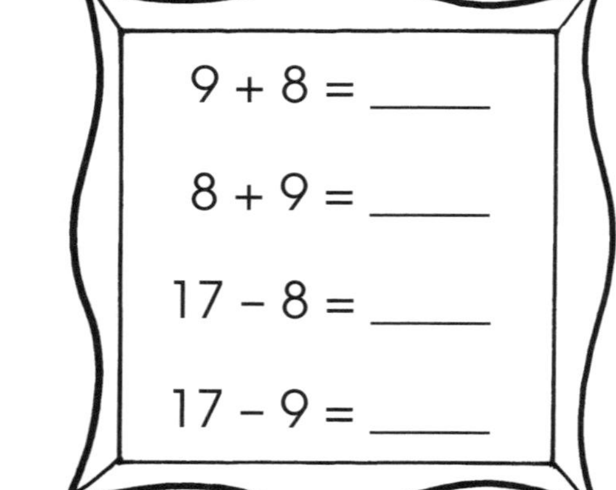

9 + 8 = _____

8 + 9 = _____

17 – 8 = _____

17 – 9 = _____

E.

6 + 3 = _____

3 + 6 = _____

9 – 3 = _____

9 – 6 = _____

F.

7 + 6 = _____

_____ + _____ = _____

13 – 7 = _____

_____ – _____ = _____

Name ____

Clowning Around

The key words "have left" and "how many more" in word problems tell you to subtract.

Circle the key words in each story. Finish each number sentence to solve the problem.

A. Fritz is juggling 8 balls. He drops 3 balls. How many balls does he have left to juggle?

______ - ______ = ______ balls

B. Mombo has 10 stars on his right shoe. He has 5 stars on his left shoe. How many more stars are on Mombo's right shoe?

______ - ______ = ______ stars

C. There are 9 polka dots on Mimi's hat. There are 6 polka dots on Sappy's hat. How many more polka dots are on Mimi's hat?

______ - ______ = ______ polka dots

D. Bonzo has 12 balloons. Then, 6 balloons pop. How many balloons does Bonzo have left?

______ - ______ = ______ balloons

Subtraction word problems

Name ______________________

Math Stories

Write a number sentence to solve each math story.

A. Trent has 15 math problems for homework. He finishes 8 problems. How many problems does Trent have left?

_____ - _____ = _____ problems

B. Juan checked out 10 books from the library. He returned 5 books. How many books does Juan have left?

_____ - _____ = _____ books

C. Shameka found 12 rocks for the science project. Emily found 8 rocks. How many more rocks did Shameka find?

_____ - _____ = _____ rocks

D. Mr. Miller's class has 18 words on their spelling test. Miss Frank's class has 9 words. How many more words does Mr. Miller's class have?

_____ - _____ = _____ words

Addition and subtraction word problems

Name ______________________________

Read Carefully

Circle the number sentence that solves each problem. Solve. Be sure to write the unit with the answer.

A. There are 7  sleeping under the rock. There are 9  crawling across the sand. How many  are there altogether?

7 + 9 = ______ 9 – 7 = ______

B. Nancy counts 12  buzzing around the flowers. Then, 5  fly away. How many  are left?

12 + 5 = ______ 12 – 5 = ______

C. At the park, 8  march onto the blanket looking for food. Then, 7  march away carrying some crumbs. How many  are left?

8 + 7 = ______ 8 – 7 = ______

D. Jerome watches 6  crawl along the path. Then, he sees 4  by the river. How many  does he see in all?

6 + 4 = ______ 6 – 4 = ______

E. There are 16  croaking. There are 8  frogs jumping. How many more  are croaking?

16 + 8 = ______ 16 – 8 = ______

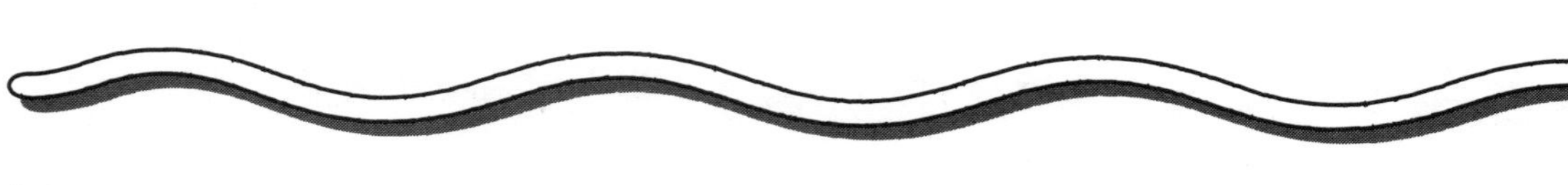

Groups of tens and ones

Name ______________________________

Lots of Drops

Circle each group of 10 raindrops. Then, draw a line to the correct number.

A. 

12

B.

15

C. 

18

D.

20

E. 

11

F.

14

G. 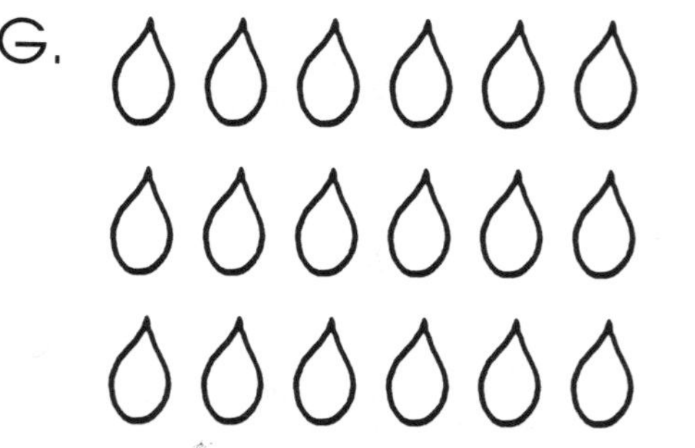

10

H.

16

List the numbers above from least to greatest.

_____, _____, _____, _____, _____, _____, _____, _____

Groups of tens and ones

Name ______________________________

Plenty of Popcorn

tens	ones
1	2

Count the groups of tens and ones. Write the number.

A. 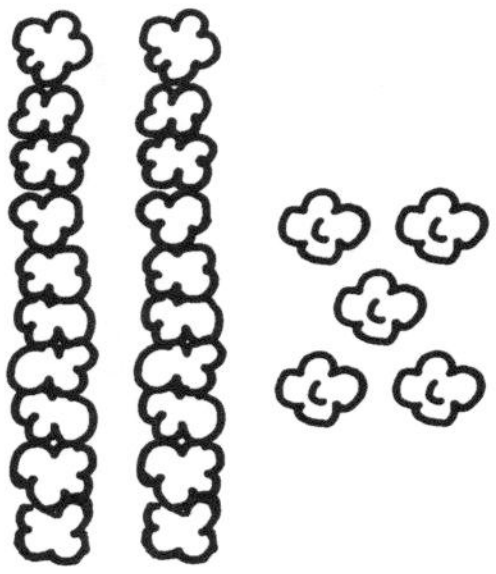 tens ______ ones ______

B.  tens ______ ones ______

C.  tens ______ ones ______

D.  tens ______ ones ______

E.  tens ______ ones ______

F.  tens ______ ones ______

G.  tens ______ ones ______

H.  tens ______ ones ______

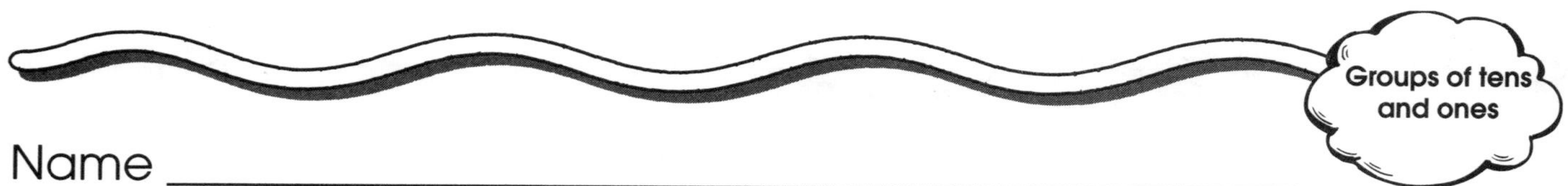

Name ___________________________________

Box It Up

Circle the correct number of blocks to match the number on each gift.

A. 57

B. 48

C. 60

D. 81

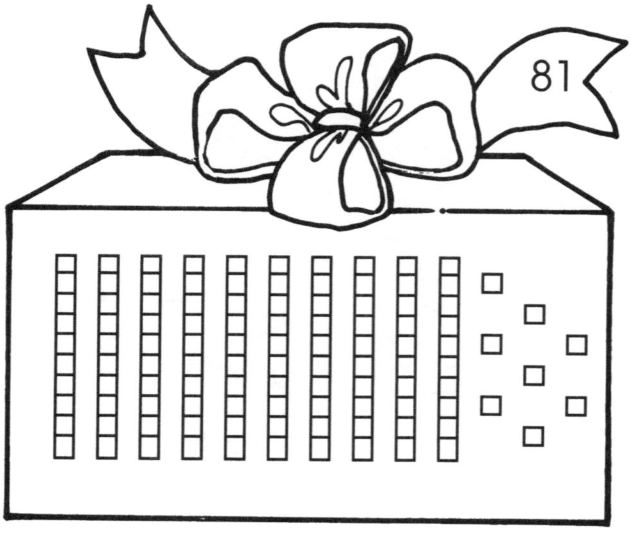

E. 25

F. 36

Name ___________________________________

Name That Number

Write each number.

A. 5 tens 4 ones = ______

B. 2 tens 7 ones = ______

C. 8 tens 9 ones = ______

D. 7 tens 5 ones = ______

E. 1 ten 6 ones = ______

F. 4 ten 3 ones = ______

G. 6 tens 0 ones = ______

H. 9 tens 1 one = ______

I. 0 tens 8 ones = ______

J. 3 tens 2 ones = ______

Write the numbers above in order from greatest to least.

____, ____, ____, ____, ____, ____, ____, ____, ____, ____

Write the number of tens and ones for each number.

K. 71 = ______ tens ______ ones

L. 58 = ______ tens ______ ones

M. 5 = ______ tens ______ ones

N. 40 = ______ tens ______ ones

Name ______________________________

Math Laugh

Write the number for each group of blocks. Then, use the code to answer the riddle.

Why does a math teacher comb her hair?

To get out the ___ ___ ___ ___ ___ ___ ___ ___ ___ ___!
37 64 73 45 20 35 28 54 82 15

A.

_____ → **T**

_____ → **G**

_____ → **E**

B.

_____ → **E**

_____ → **R**

_____ → **S**

C.

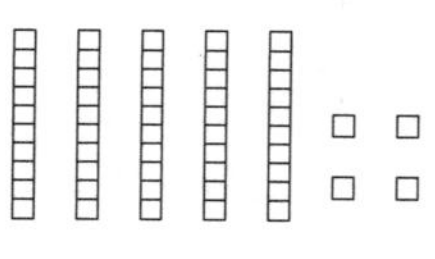

_____ → **L**

_____ → **C**

D.

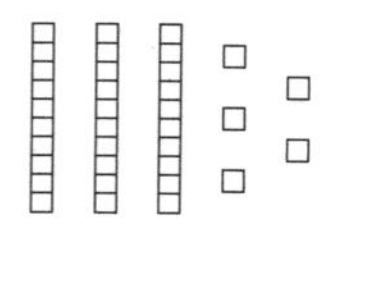

_____ → **N**

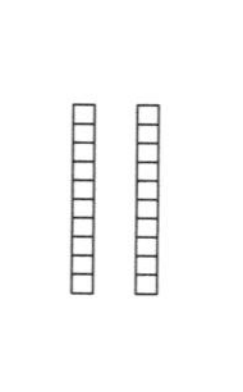

_____ → **A**

Name ______________________________________

Stack It Up

Add 10 blocks to each group. Write the new number.

A. 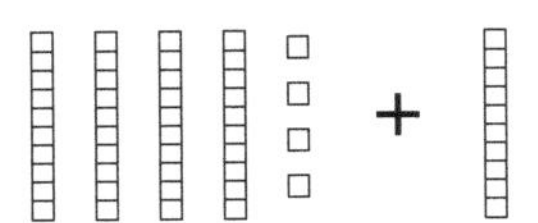

_______ + _______ = _______

B. 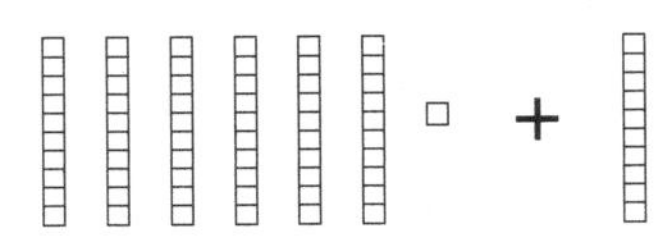

_______ + _______ = _______

C. 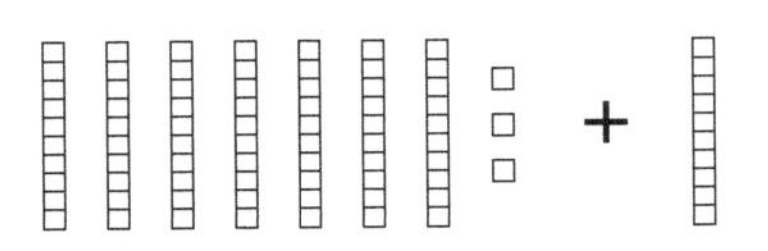

_______ + _______ = _______

D. 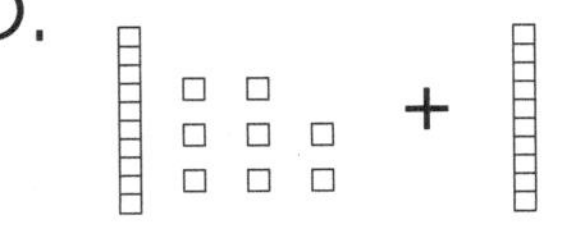

_______ + _______ = _______

E.

_______ + _______ = _______

F. 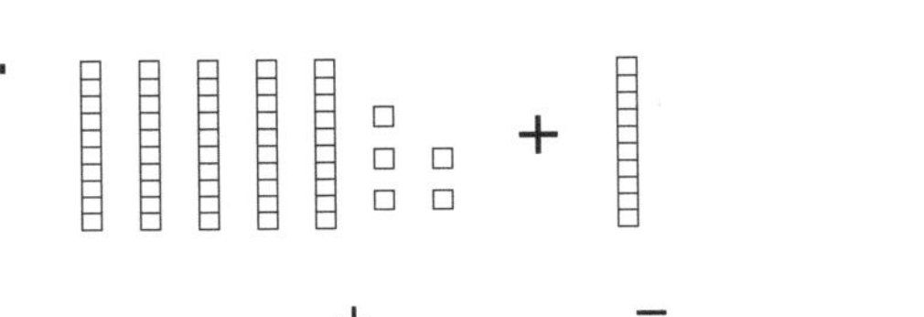

_______ + _______ = _______

Complete the table by adding 10 to each number on the left.

+ 10	
62	
33	
87	
5	
56	
21	

Name ____

Planting Seeds

Take 10 seeds away from each picture. Write the number.

A. 

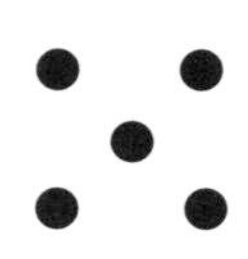

35 – 10 = ______

B. 

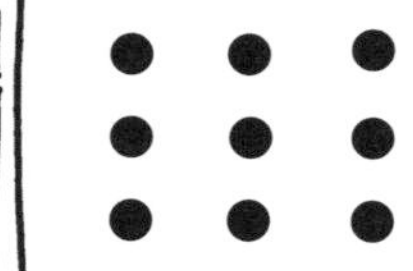

59 – 10 = ______

C. 

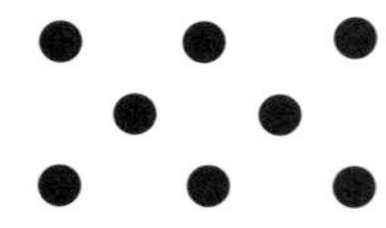

18 – 10 = ______

D. 

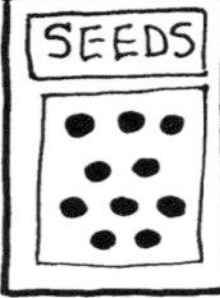

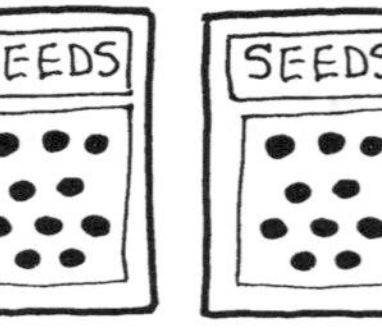

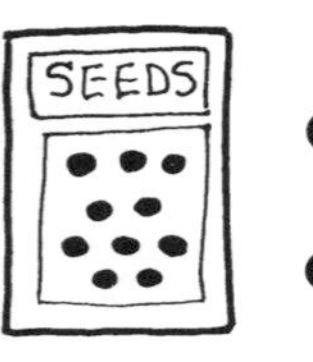

62 – 10 = ______

E. 

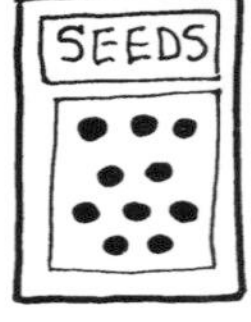

70 – 10 = ______

F. 

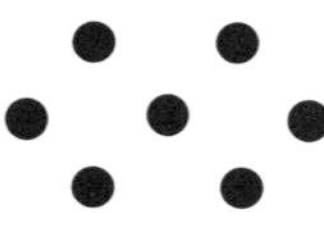
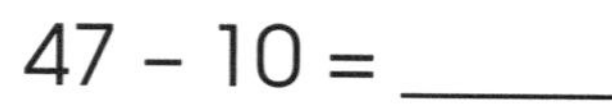

47 – 10 = ______

Name ______________________________

Put It Together

Putting 10 tens together makes 1 hundred.

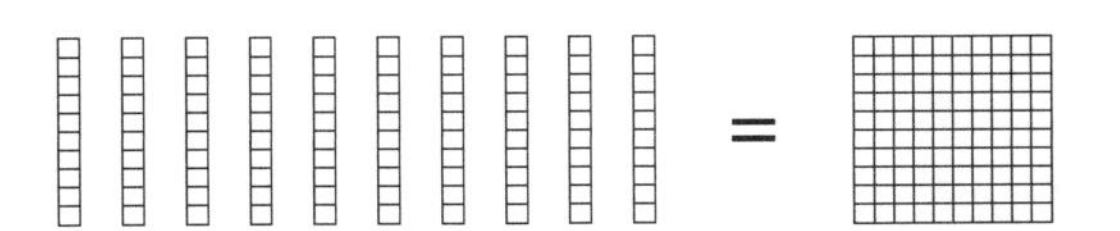

Count each group of blocks. Write the number of hundreds, tens, and ones.

A. 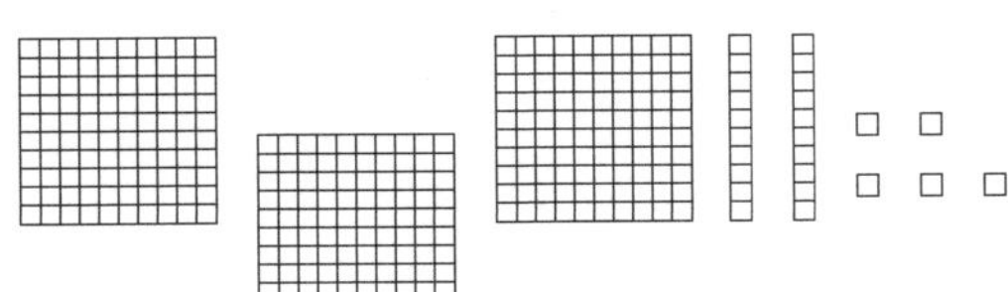 =

hundreds	tens	ones
______	______	______

B. 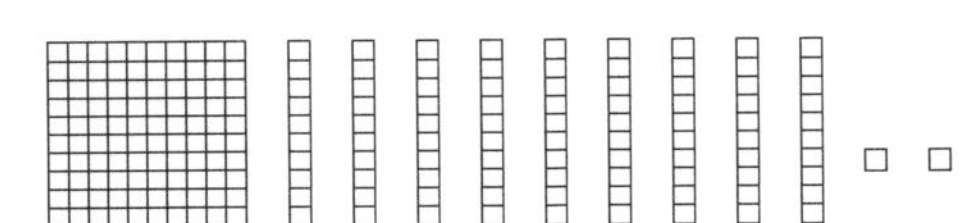 =

hundreds	tens	ones
______	______	______

C. 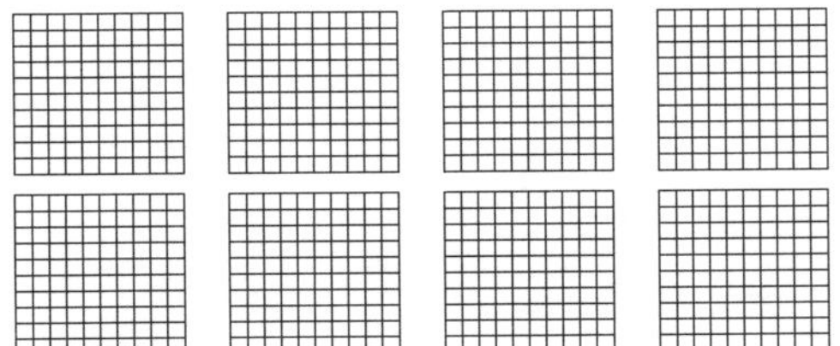 =

hundreds	tens	ones
______	______	______

D. 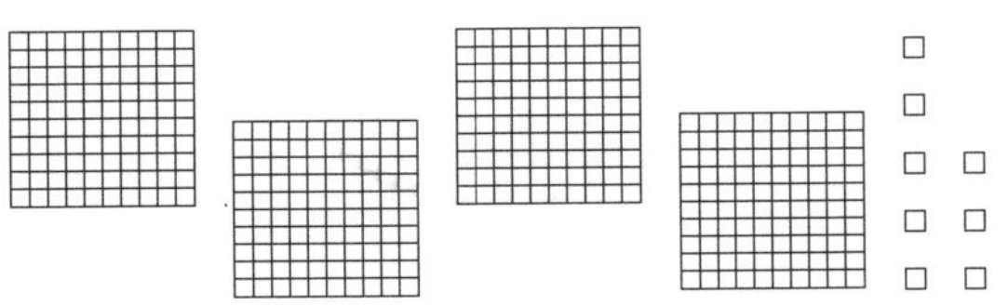 =

hundreds	tens	ones
______	______	______

E. 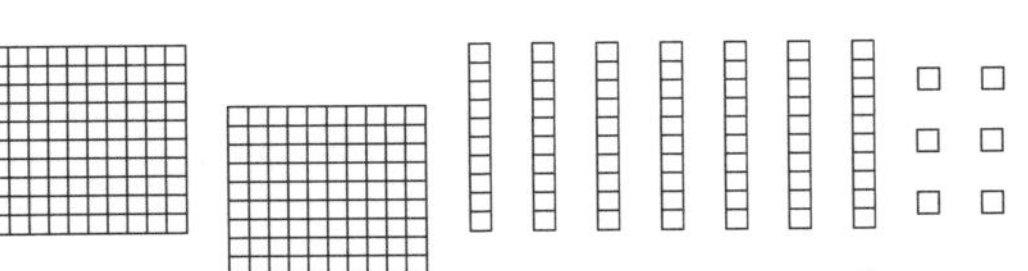 =

hundreds	tens	ones
______	______	______

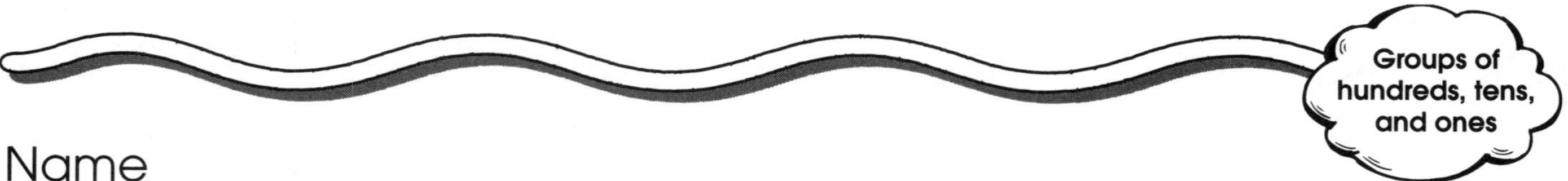

Name ____________________

Lots of Color

Draw Xs on the blocks to show each number.

A.

H	T	O
2	6	1

= 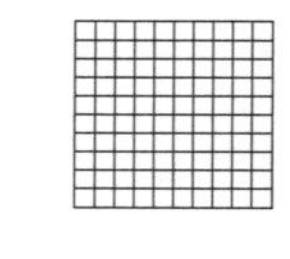 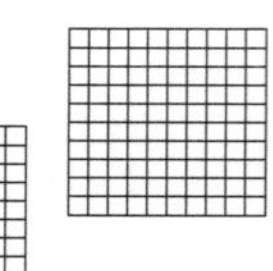 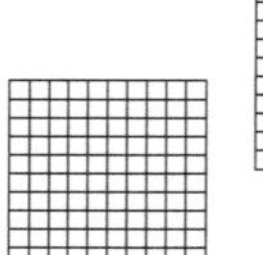 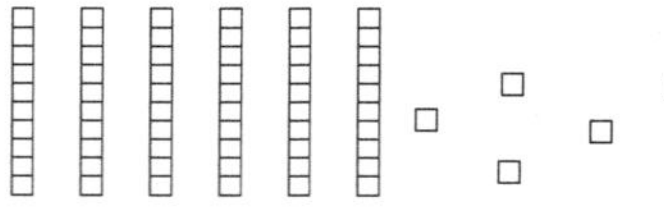

B.

H	T	O
4	2	8

= 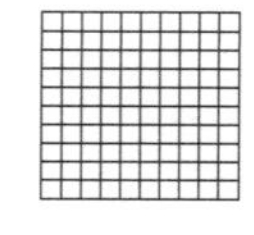 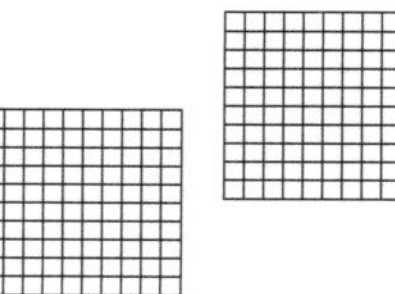 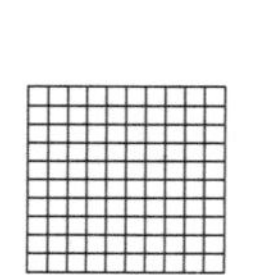 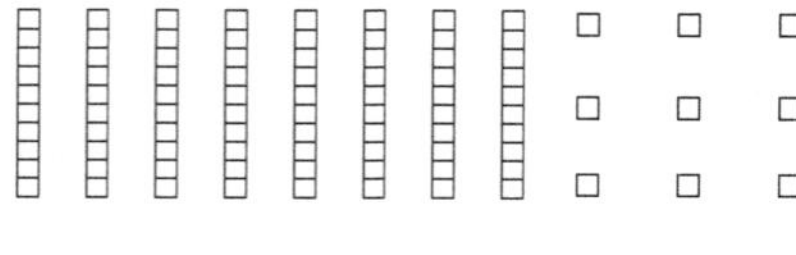

C.

H	T	O
5	3	4

= 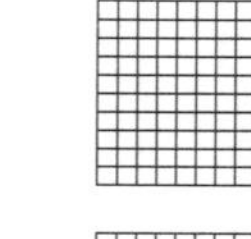 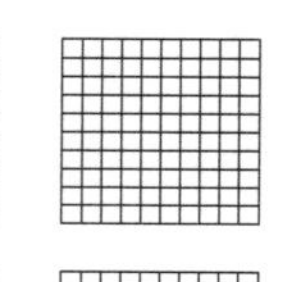 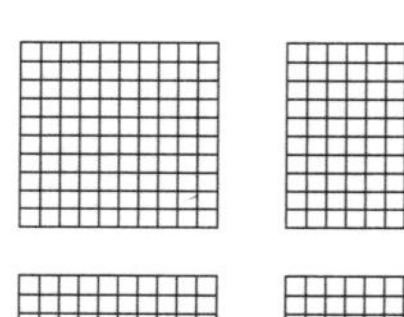 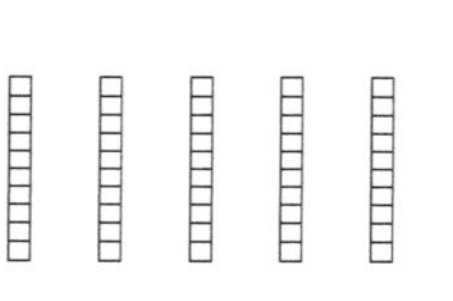

D.

H	T	O
1	7	0

= 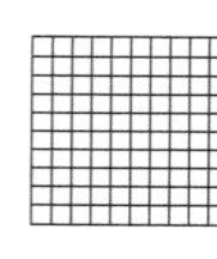 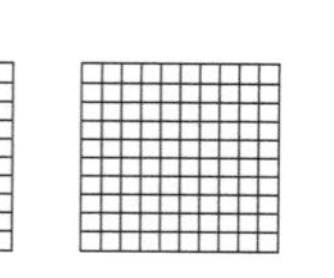 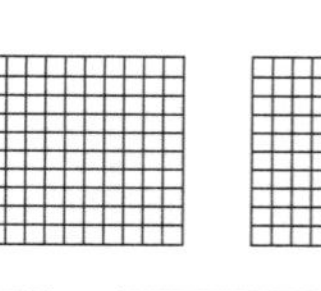 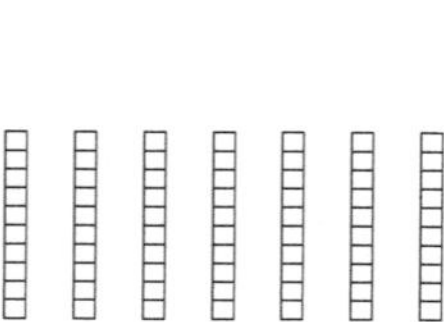

E.

H	T	O
6	0	6

= 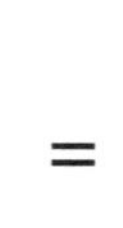 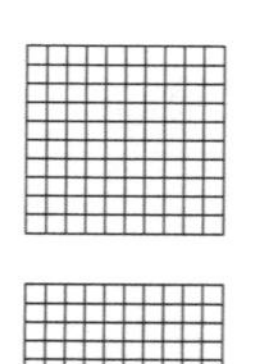 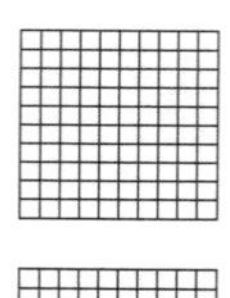 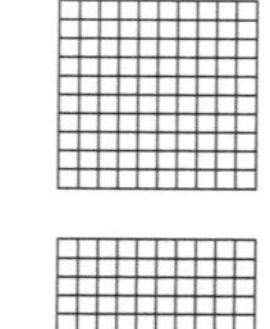 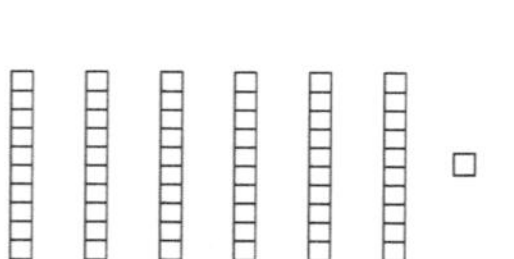 

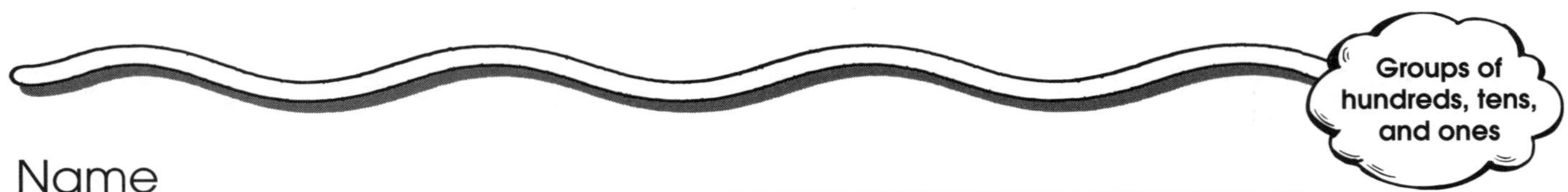

Name ______________________________

Fill It Up

Use each chart to write the number on the gas pump.

A.

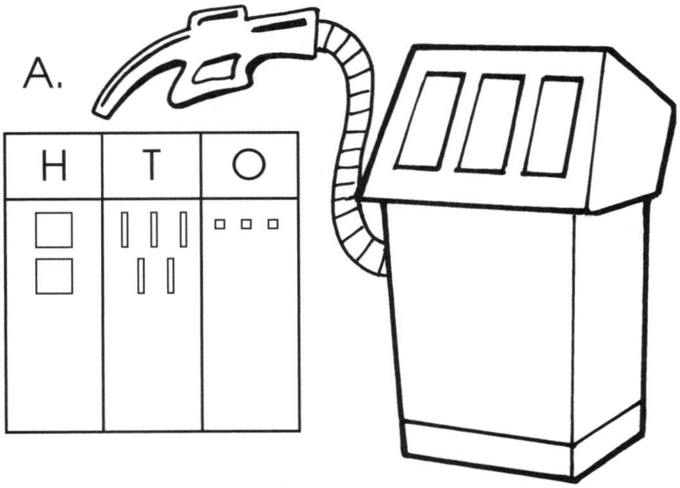

H	T	O

B.

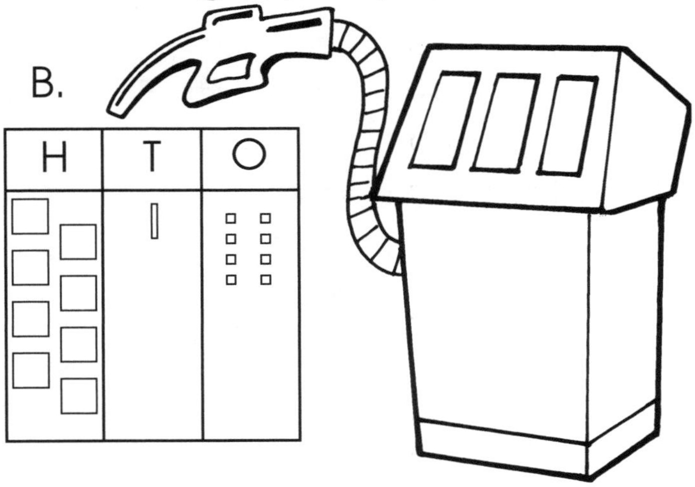

H	T	O

C.

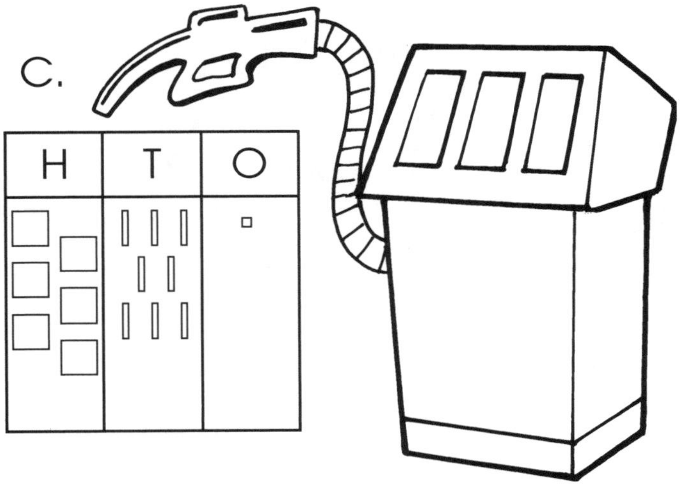

H	T	O

D.

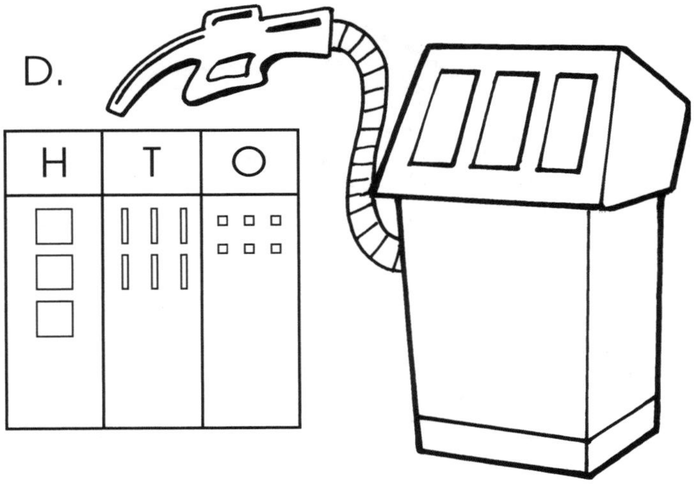

H	T	O

E.

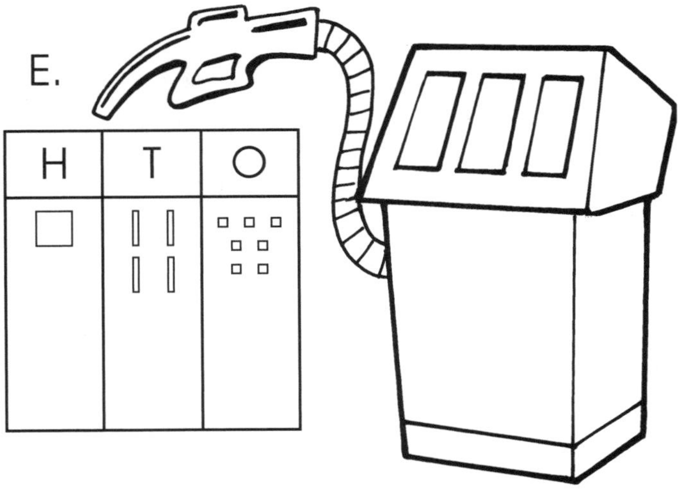

H	T	O

F.

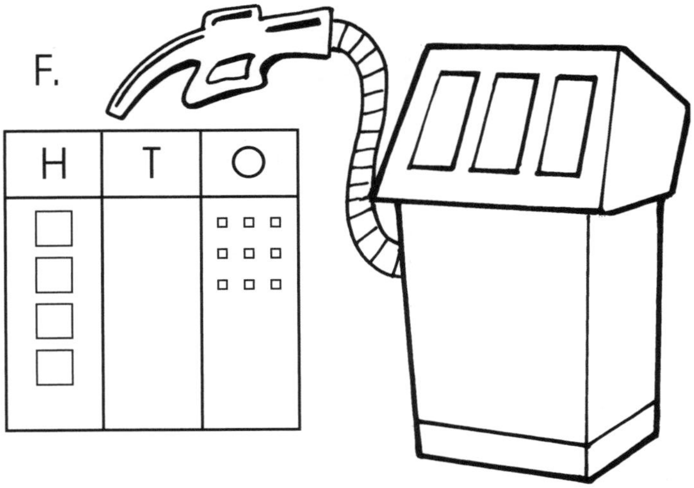

H	T	O

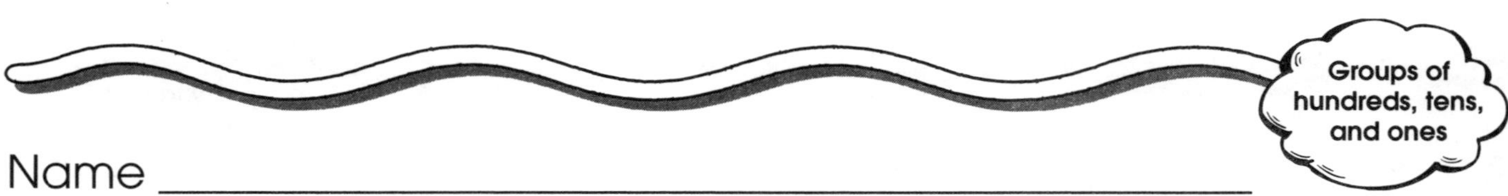

Name ______________________________

Jelly Beans

Use the code to color the jar of jelly beans.

Color the jelly beans with 2 hundreds orange.
Color the jelly beans with 5 hundreds green.
Color the jelly beans with 3 tens red.
Color the jelly beans with 7 tens yellow.
Color the jelly beans with 9 ones purple.
Color the jelly beans with 6 ones blue.

133 263 756
974 409 886 672
528 240 632 375
169 834 319 293
936 446 565 378
512 133 251

How many jelly beans have a number greater than 500? _____

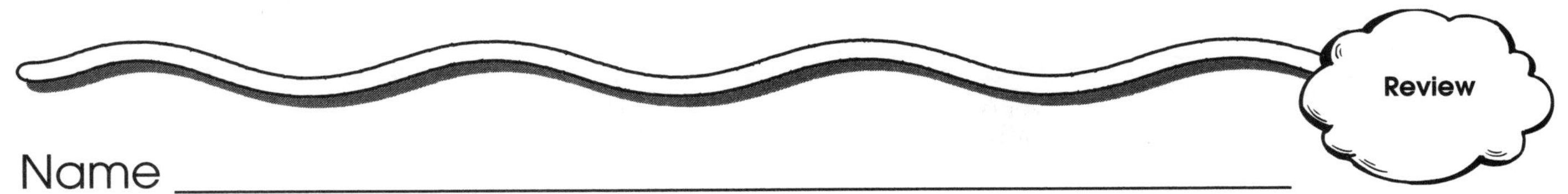

Name ____________________

Time to Review

Numeration, Comparing Numbers,
Addition and Subtraction Facts, Place Value

Circle the number of stars in each picture.

A.

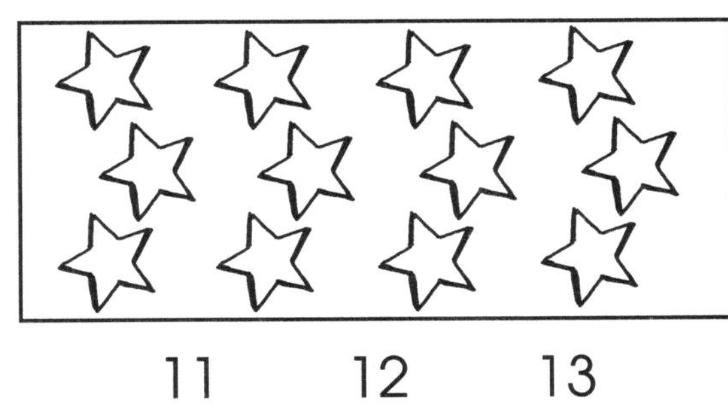

11 12 13

B.

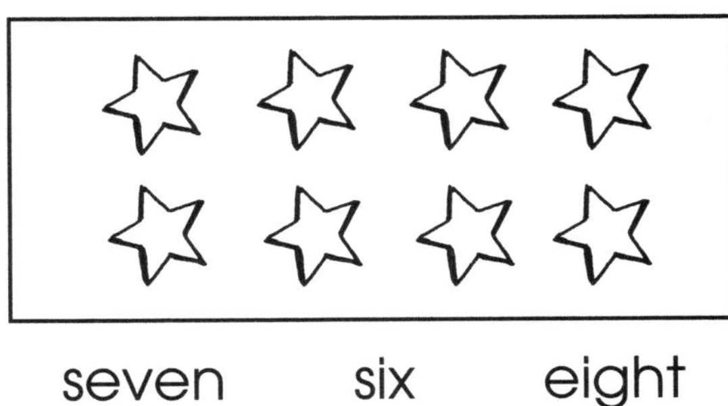

seven six eight

C. Count by ones. Write each missing number.

79, ______, 81, 82, 83, ______, ______, ______, ______, ______, ______

D. Count back by ones. Write each missing number.

36, 35, 34, 33, ______, ______, ______, ______, ______, ______, ______

Write each missing number.

E. Count by 2s.

F. Count by 5s.

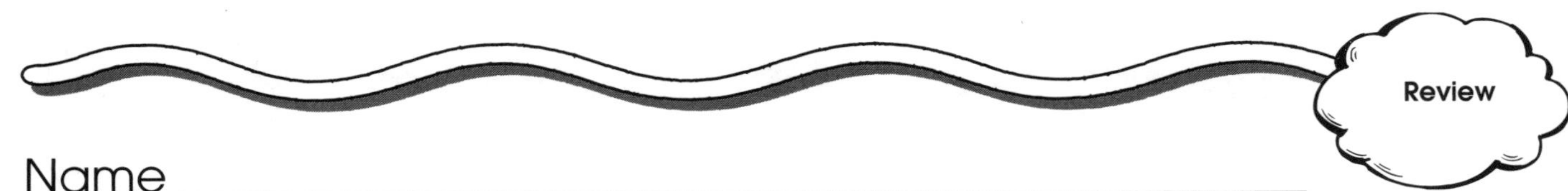

Name ____________________

Circle the number that is less.

G. 21 19

H. 41 43

Write **>** or **<** in the circle.

I. 83 ◯ 89

J. 30 ◯ 28

Write each group of numbers from least to greatest.

K. 63 13 36 _____ _____ _____

L. 40 34 25 _____ _____ _____

Fill in the circle for the correct number.

M. I am an even number less than 24.

28	21	18
◯	◯	◯

N. I am an odd number between 32 and 37.

35	39	32
◯	◯	◯

Write a number sentence to solve the word problem.

O. Fritz finished 15 math problems on Friday and 8 problems on Saturday. How many more problems did Fritz finish on Friday?

Name ______________________________

Circle the bird that is sixth in line.

P.

Solve.

Q. $5 + 7 =$ ______ $8 +$ ______ $= 14$ $13 - 4 =$ ______

R. $4 +$ ______ $= 6$ $12 - 4 =$ ______ $14 -$ ______ $= 7$

S.

4	17	9	6	15
+ 6	− 9	+ 3	+ 7	− 8

Write two facts that equal 6.

T. ______ + ______ = 6 ______ − ______ = 6

Write each number.

U. = ________

V. = ________

Write the number that is 10 less.

W. − = ________

Name ______________________________

Strike

First, add the ones.
Then, add the tens.

	T	O
	2	6
+	3	1
	5	7

Which bowling pin will fall next? To find out, solve the problems in each row. Cross off each sum on the bowling pins. The bowling pin with all the numbers crossed off is the next one to fall. Color it.

A.

$$\begin{array}{r} 43 \\ +\ 52 \\ \hline \end{array} \qquad \begin{array}{r} 16 \\ +\ 33 \\ \hline \end{array} \qquad \begin{array}{r} 71 \\ +\ 8 \\ \hline \end{array} \qquad \begin{array}{r} 24 \\ +\ 14 \\ \hline \end{array} \qquad \begin{array}{r} 85 \\ +\ 3 \\ \hline \end{array}$$

B.

$$\begin{array}{r} 39 \\ +\ 20 \\ \hline \end{array} \qquad \begin{array}{r} 15 \\ +\ 41 \\ \hline \end{array} \qquad \begin{array}{r} 46 \\ +\ 32 \\ \hline \end{array} \qquad \begin{array}{r} 57 \\ +\ 32 \\ \hline \end{array} \qquad \begin{array}{r} 93 \\ +\ 4 \\ \hline \end{array}$$

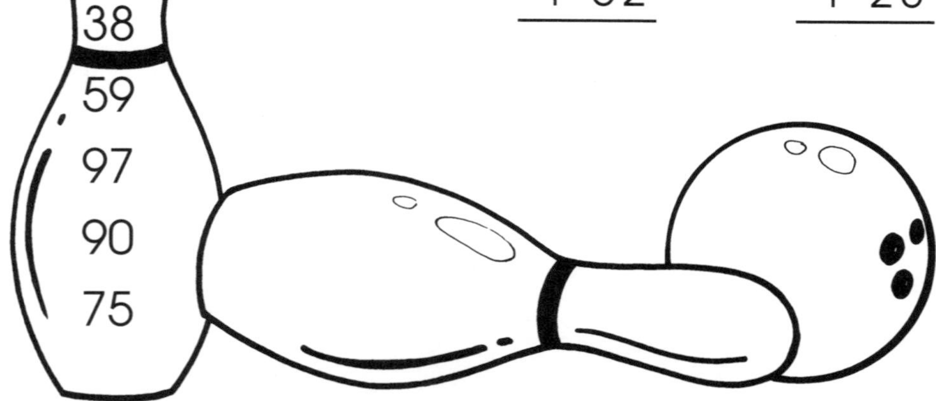

C.

$$\begin{array}{r} 24 \\ +\ 62 \\ \hline \end{array} \qquad \begin{array}{r} 73 \\ +\ 23 \\ \hline \end{array}$$

Adding 2-digit numbers with no regrouping

Name ____________________

Compare the Pair

Solve. Compare each sum. Write **>**, **<**, or **=** in the circle.

A. 54 + 25 ◯ 63 + 16

B. 43 + 35 ◯ 51 + 17

C. 36 + 22 ◯ 48 + 11

D. 24 + 44 ◯ 16 + 52

E. 17 + 70 ◯ 64 + 25

F. 75 + 12 ◯ 81 + 3

Adding 2-digit numbers with no regrouping

Name ______________________________

The Missing Piece

Write each missing addend.

A.

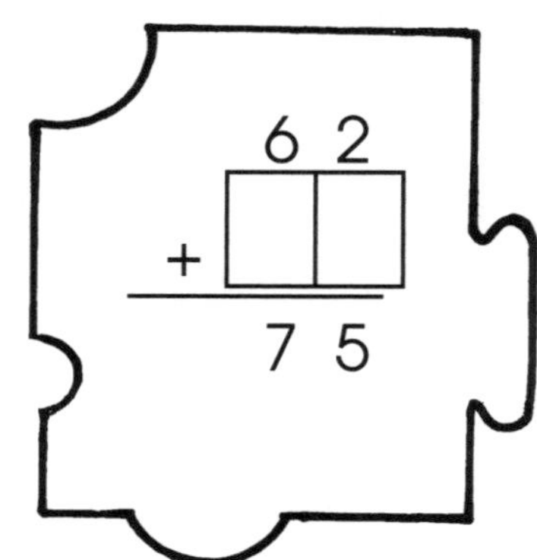

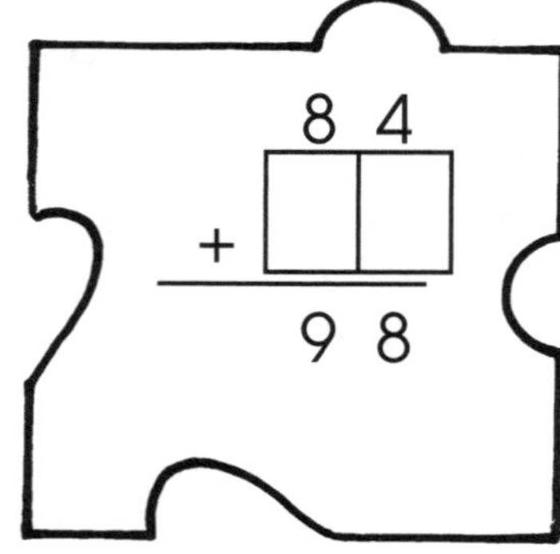

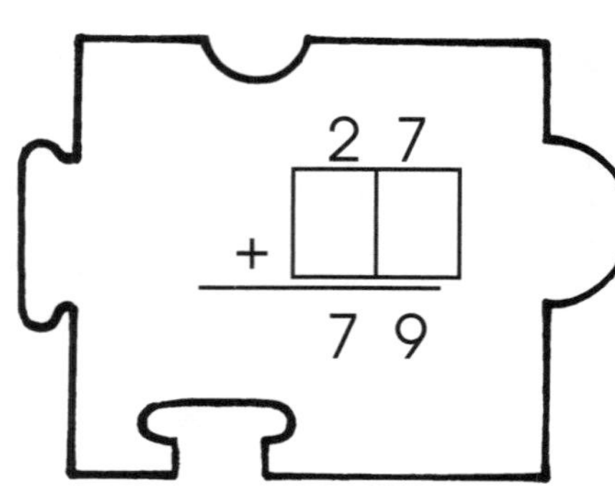

B.

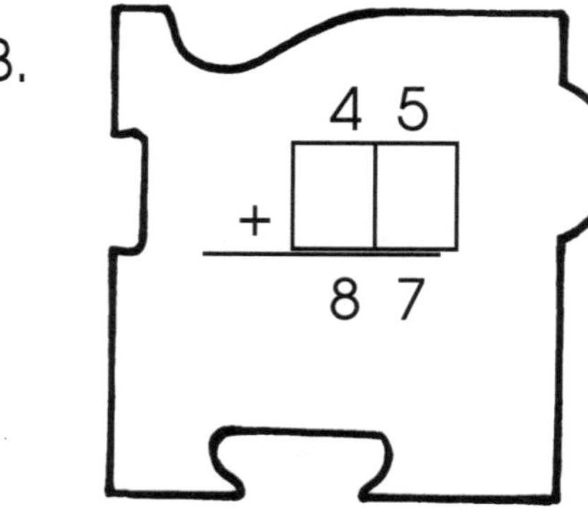

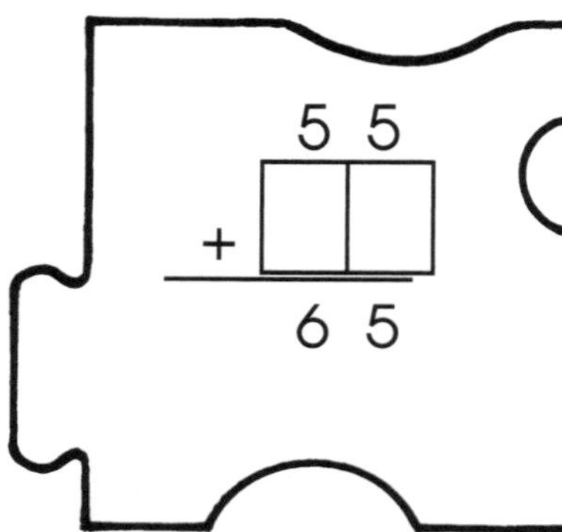

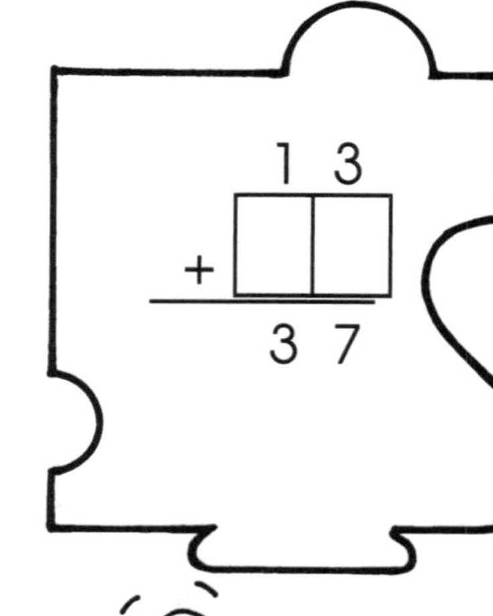

C.

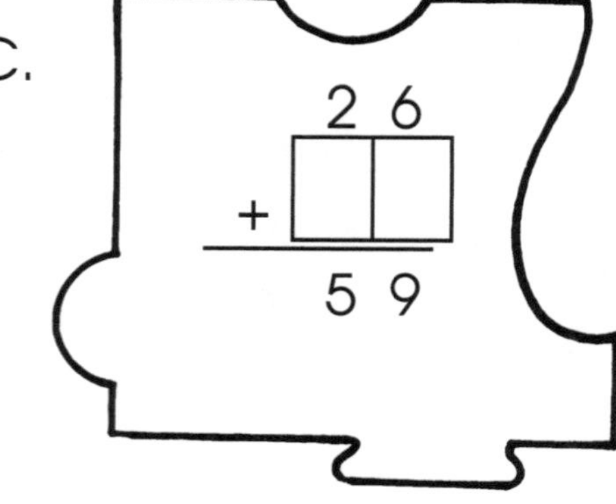

9 1
+ ☐☐
9 6

Write the addends for the sum.

☐☐
+ ☐☐
8 4

Name ________________________________

Flower Power

First, add the ones.
Then, add the tens.
Last, add the hundreds.

	H	T	O
	2	5	3
+	1	3	6
	3	8	9

Add. Write each sum in the puzzle.

Across

A. 621 + 237

C. 345 + 312

Down

A. 563 + 313

B. 404 + 473

A.		B.
	■	
C.		

A.		B.
	■	
C.		

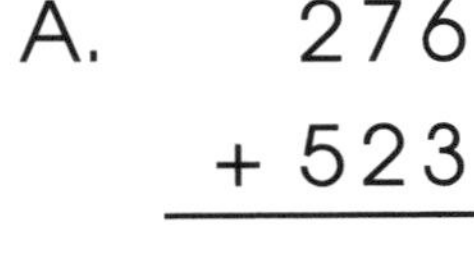

Across

A. 276 + 523

C. 823 + 122

Down

A. 129 + 640

B. 250 + 745

Regrouping from ones to tens

Name ____

Ready to Regroup

Regrouping means to take 10 ones to make another ten. This is how it works.

I have 25 beads. I find 6 more. How many beads do I have in all?

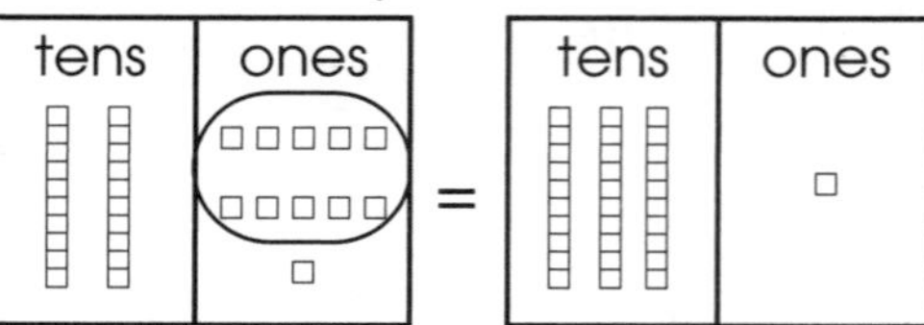

Regroup 10 ones as 1 ten.
I have 31 beads.

Regroup to solve each problem.

A. I have 36 beads. | I find 6 more. | How many beads in all? | I have ____ beads.

tens | ones

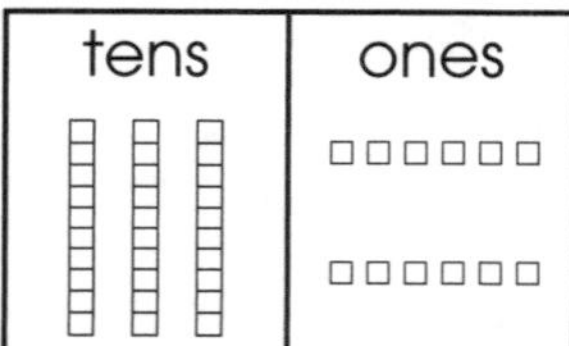

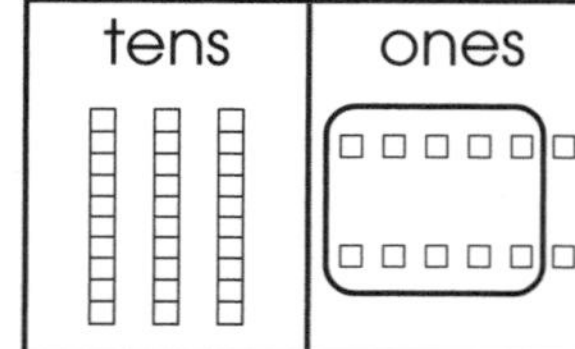

tens | ones

B. I have 18 beads. | I find 5 more. | How many beads in all? | I have ____ beads.

tens | ones

tens | ones

C. I have 28 beads. | I find 6 more. | How many beads in all? | I have ____ beads.

tens | ones

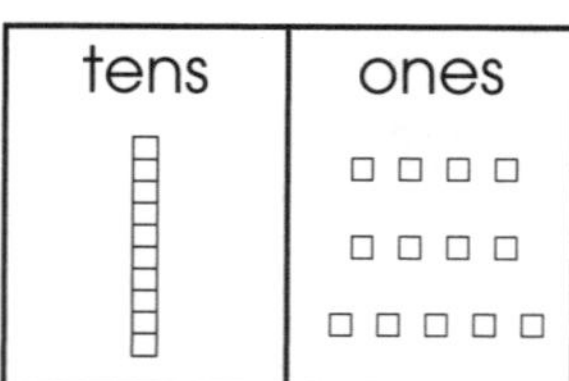

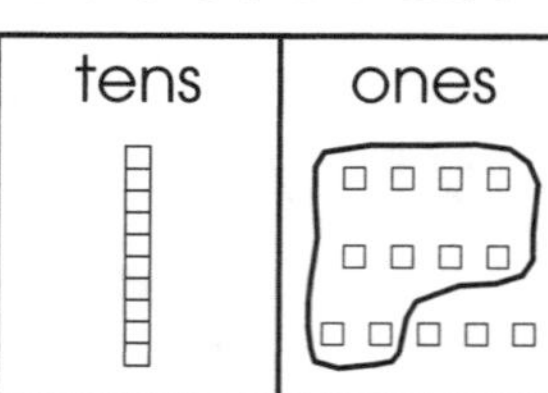

tens | ones

Adding with regrouping

Name ______________________________

Catch the Sum!

Use these steps to add and regroup.

1. Add the ones.
   6 + 8 = 14 ones
   Regroup before you add the tens.

tens	ones
☐	
2	6
+	8

2. Regroup 14 ones as 1 ten and 4 ones.
   Write 4 ones in the sum.
   Write 1 in the tens column.

tens	ones
1	
2	6
+	8
	4

The sum is 34.

3. Add the tens.
   1 + 2 = 3 tens
   Write 3 tens in the sum.

tens	ones
1	
2	6
+	8
3	4

Add.

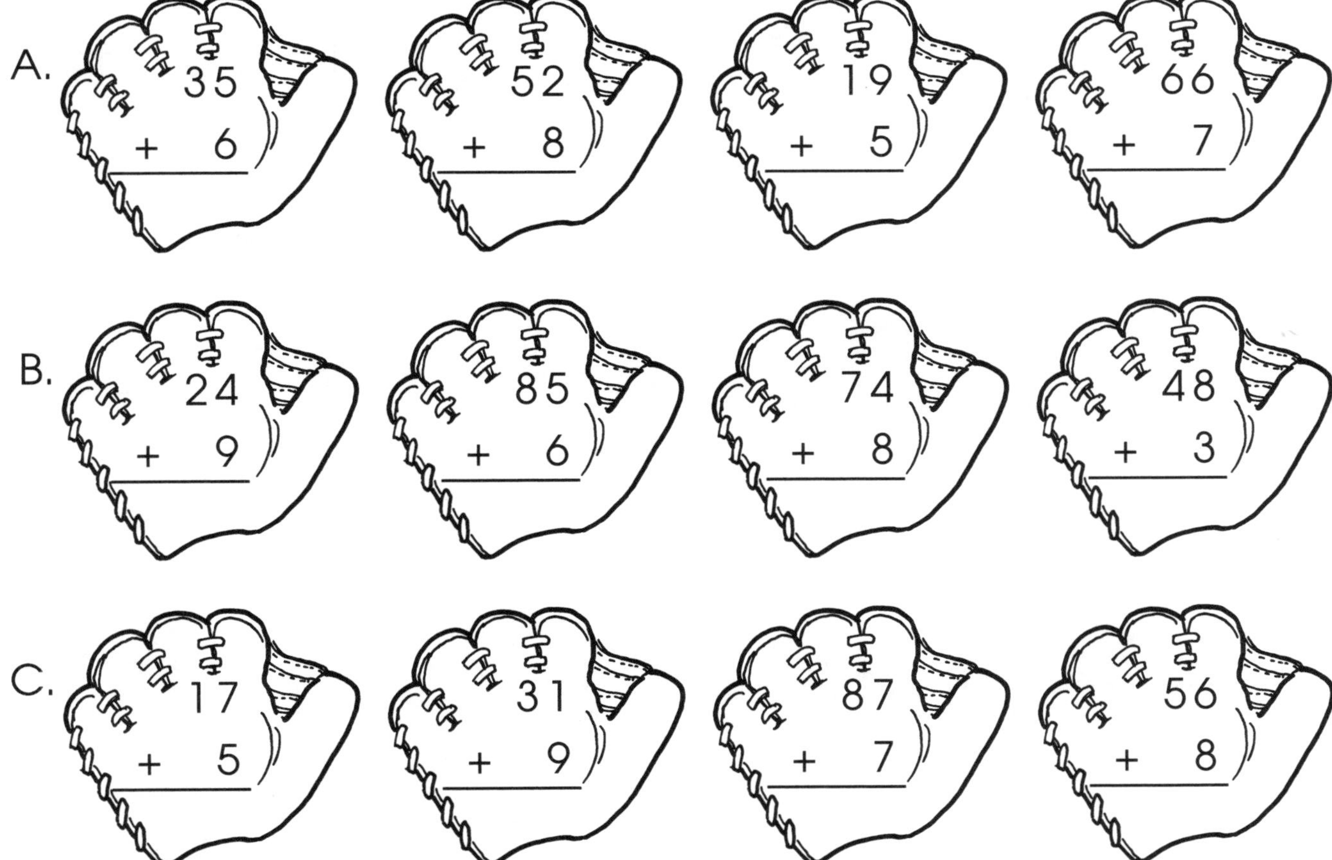

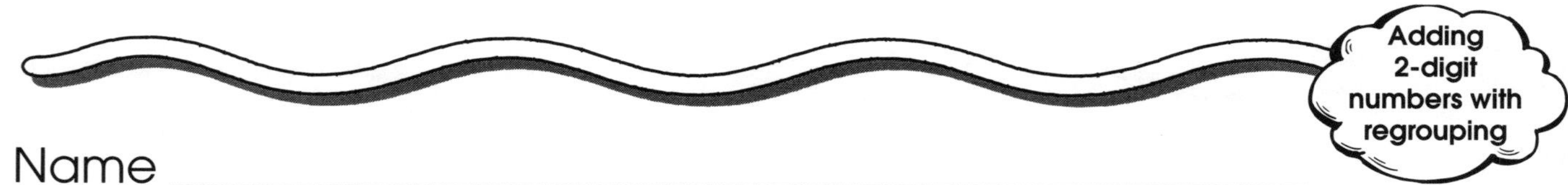

Adding 2-digit numbers with regrouping

Name ______________________________

Flying Fast

Add. Then, use the code to find the answer to the question.

What are the fastest flying insects?

___	___	___	___	___	___	___	___	___	___	___
52	32	94	71	88	81	93	65	77	96	90

A $68 + 26$	**G** $42 + 29$	**S** $63 + 27$	**F** $55 + 38$
E $79 + 17$	**O** $39 + 49$	**I** $48 + 29$	
D $37 + 15$	**N** $54 + 27$		
L $26 + 39$	**R** $14 + 18$		

Adding 2-digit numbers with regrouping

Name ______________________________

What a Treat!

Look at this!

	tens	ones
	[1]	
	7	3
+	2	9
1	0	2

1 ten + 9 tens = 10 tens

Starting with row A, add the problems in order. Cross out each sum on the frozen ice-cream treats to see which treat is finished first.

A.

56	59	29	79	35
+ 28	+ 39	+ 49	+ 29	+ 36

B.

47	12	72	57
+ 25	+ 18	+ 39	+ 17

C.

94	49	63
+ 56	+ 76	+ 88

D.

54	25	92
+ 67	+ 45	+ 38

78
71
72
111
74
150
70
87

84
98
108
30
125
151
121
130

Adding three 2-digit numbers

Name ____

Three Sums in a Row

Add each problem in order. Then, mark an **X** or **O** in the puzzle below to find three **X**s or **O**s in a row.

A.
```
  32
  15
+ 26
```
Mark X.

B.
```
  44
  21
+ 50
```
Mark O.

C.
```
  17
  33
+ 18
```
Mark X.

D.
```
  25
  16
+ 64
```
Mark O.

E.
```
  19
  41
+ 22
```
Mark X.

F.
```
  75
  25
+ 23
```
Mark O.

G.
```
  51
  42
+ 33
```
Mark X.

H.
```
  60
  17
+ 26
```
Mark O.

I.
```
  29
  12
+ 53
```
Mark X.

68	126	103
82	105	94
123	73	115

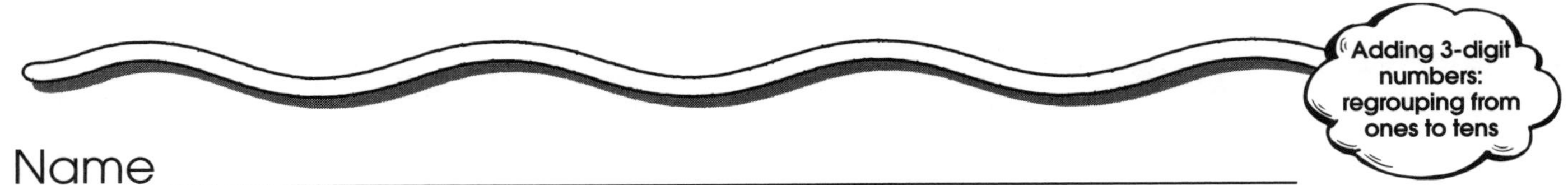

Name ______________________________

Smooth Landing

Add. Then, color each cloud with an even-numbered sum to land the airplane.

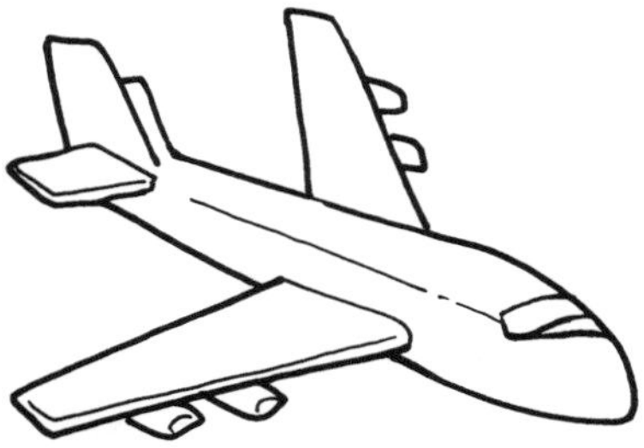

	156 + 328	264 + 717	534 + 349
214 + 657	352 + 529	246 + 446	687 + 103
345 + 338	207 + 569	436 + 124	649 + 223
757 + 218	219 + 179	325 + 626	508 + 453
548 + 129	201 + 279	128 + 438	

Name ________________________________

Three Cheers

Use these steps to regroup from the tens to the hundreds.

1. Add the ones. $2 + 4 = 6$
2. Add the tens. 7 tens + 5 tens = 12 tens
3. Regroup. 12 tens = 1 hundred and 2 tens
4. Add the hundreds.
   1 hundred + 3 hundreds + 2 hundreds = 6 hundreds

	H	T	O
	[1]		
	3	7	2
+	2	5	4
	6	2	6

Add.

A. $\begin{array}{r} 486 \\ +\ 352 \\ \hline \end{array}$ $\begin{array}{r} 173 \\ +\ 594 \\ \hline \end{array}$ $\begin{array}{r} 631 \\ +\ 182 \\ \hline \end{array}$

B. $\begin{array}{r} 260 \\ +\ 478 \\ \hline \end{array}$ $\begin{array}{r} 785 \\ +\ 144 \\ \hline \end{array}$ $\begin{array}{r} 573 \\ +\ 262 \\ \hline \end{array}$

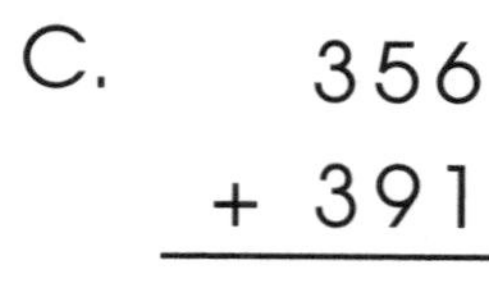

C. $\begin{array}{r} 356 \\ +\ 391 \\ \hline \end{array}$ $\begin{array}{r} 659 \\ +\ 250 \\ \hline \end{array}$ $\begin{array}{r} 486 \\ +\ 373 \\ \hline \end{array}$

D. $\begin{array}{r} 745 \\ +\ 171 \\ \hline \end{array}$ $\begin{array}{r} 562 \\ +\ 382 \\ \hline \end{array}$ $\begin{array}{r} 273 \\ +\ 295 \\ \hline \end{array}$

Adding 3-digit numbers with regrouping twice

Name ______________________________

You Are a Star

Sometimes you will need to regroup the ones and the tens.

Add.

A.	653 + 187	496 + 375	568 + 239	342 + 178
B.	536 + 198	787 + 167	465 + 398	614 + 289
C.	159 + 163	346 + 578	597 + 246	488 + 393
D.	587 + 374	264 + 168	492 + 259	679 + 251

Choose five sums from above. List them from greatest to least.

__________, __________, __________, __________, __________

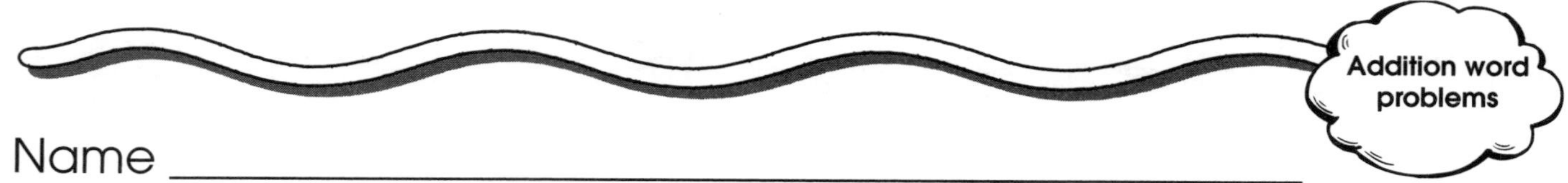

Name ____

Travel Time

Write an addition problem for each story. Solve. Label the answer with the story unit.

A. The Mason family drove 256 miles on Thursday and 315 miles on Friday. How many miles did they drive altogether?

+ ______

B. While they were driving, Carly read 26 pages in the morning and 17 pages in the afternoon. The next day she read 31 pages. How many pages did Carly read in all?

+ ______

C. Justin played with his handheld game. In the first game, he scored 496 points. In the next game, he scored 468 points. How many points did he score altogether?

+ ______

D. Carly and Justin counted cars for 30 minutes. Carly counted 49 white cars. Justin counted 51 blue cars. How many cars did they count altogether?

+ ______

Subtracting 2-digit numbers with no regrouping

Name ______________________________

Hop to Work

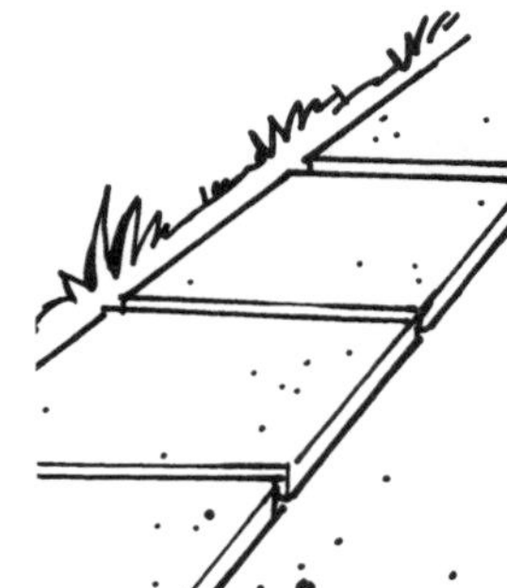

Follow these steps to subtract 2-digit numbers.

1. Subtract the ones.
2. Subtract the tens.

Subtract. Then, use the code to answer the riddle.

Why did the rabbit cross the road? To get to

___ ___ ___   ___ ___ ___ ___ ___ ___ ___   ___ ___ ___ ___

33 53 44   31 10 42 15 52 24 74   32 11 43 12

H. 58 − 27 = ___

93 − 41 = ___

T. 67 − 34 = ___

86 − 12 = ___

P. 38 − 23 = ___

M. 45 − 13 = ___

E. 79 − 35 = ___

O. 26 − 16 = ___

L. 37 − 25 = ___

L. 77 − 34 = ___

H. 95 − 42 = ___

P. 64 − 22 = ___

A. 41 − 30 = ___

N. 57 − 33 = ___

Name ______________________________

A Subtraction Pattern

Subtract. Then, follow the directions below to color the squares.

A.	758 − 346	993 − 261	696 − 453	798 − 413	457 − 136
B.	985 − 421	645 − 243	287 − 135	869 − 224	972 − 651
C.	856 − 541	757 − 223	489 − 317	896 − 404	985 − 742
D.	618 − 305	569 − 235	802 − 301	672 − 240	784 − 122

Color each square with a 2 in the ones place blue.
Color each square with a 4 in the tens place red.
Color each square with a 3 in the hundreds place yellow.
Color each square with a 5 in the hundreds place green.

Write a subtraction problem. The difference should have a 6 in the tens place.

Name ______________________________

What a Snack!

There are 31 doughnuts in the box. We eat 16 of them. How many doughnuts are left?

1. Subtract the ones.

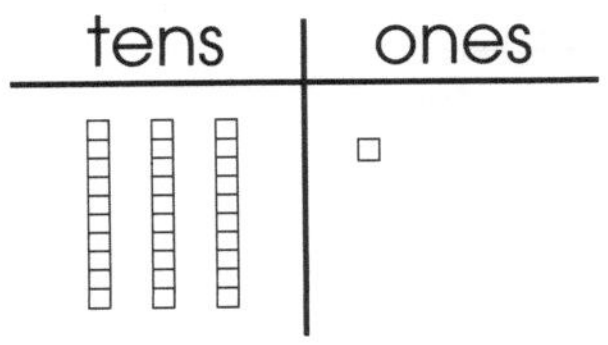


```
  31
- 16
----
```

There are not enough ones to subtract.

2. Regroup.

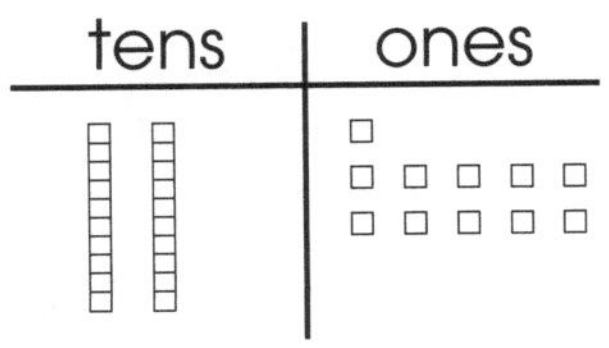


```
  2 11
  3̸ 1̸
- 1  6
------
```

3. Subtract the ones. Then, subtract the tens.

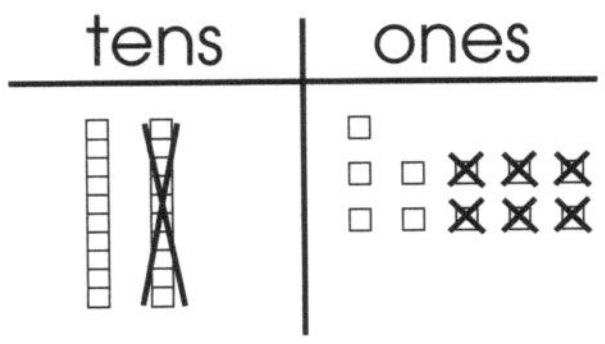


```
  2 11
  3̸ 1̸
- 1  6
------
  1  5
```

There are 15 doughnuts left.

Subtract.

A.

45	63	22	54
− 28	− 39	− 15	− 36

B.

87	30	66	71
− 48	− 17	− 9	− 63

C.

48	32	53	95
− 29	− 17	− 26	− 49

Name ______________________________

Go "Fore" It!

Round each number to the nearest ten. Estimate the difference.

A.
```
  45 → [ ]
- 12 → -[ ]
         [ ]
```

B.
```
  73 → [ ]
- 29 → -[ ]
         [ ]
```

C.
```
  68 → [ ]
- 47 → -[ ]
         [ ]
```

D.
```
  92 → [ ]
- 54 → -[ ]
         [ ]
```

E.
```
  33 → [ ]
- 18 → -[ ]
         [ ]
```

F.
```
  49 → [ ]
- 36 → -[ ]
         [ ]
```

G.
```
  24 → [ ]
- 11 → -[ ]
         [ ]
```

H.
```
  65 → [ ]
- 22 → -[ ]
         [ ]
```

Name ______________________________

Regrouping Exercise

Subtract.

A.

462	785
− 135	− 249

B.

236	683	312	895
− 118	− 359	− 204	− 537

C.

521	374	153	786
− 315	− 128	− 127	− 469

D.

690	266	478	854
− 278	− 137	− 349	− 616

E.

961	540
− 354	− 426

Subtracting 3-digit numbers: regrouping from hundreds to tens

Name ______________________________

A Long Snake

Subtract.

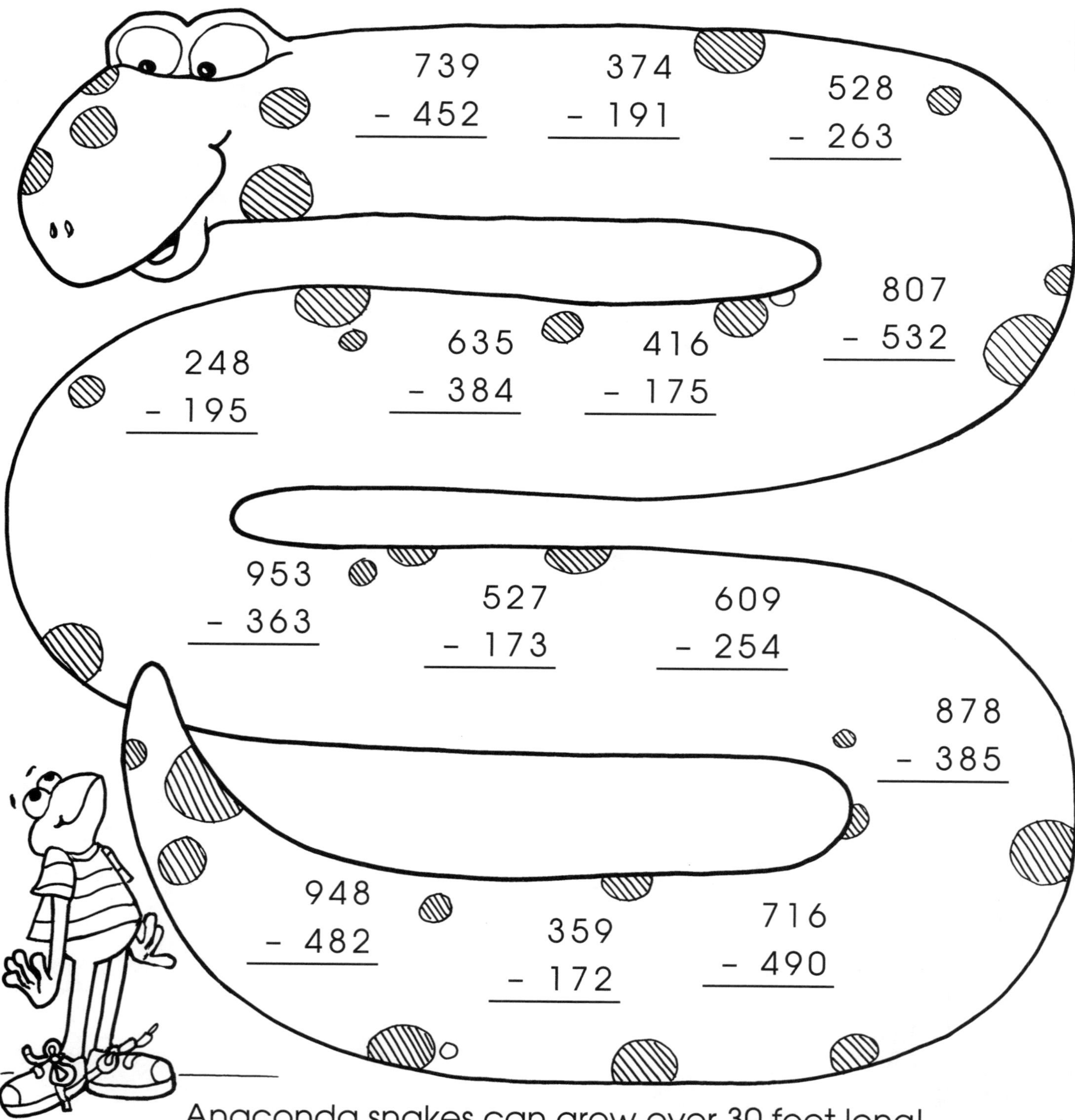

Anaconda snakes can grow over 30 feet long!

Subtracting 3-digit numbers with regrouping twice

Name ______________________________

Follow the Steps

1. Subtract the ones.	2. Regroup and subtract.	3. Subtract the tens.	4. Regroup and subtract.
351 – 186 _____ There are not enough ones to subtract.	4 11 3~~5~~~~1~~ – 186 _____ 5	4 11 3~~5~~~~1~~ – 186 _____ 5 There are not enough tens to subtract.	2 14 11 ~~3~~~~5~~~~1~~ – 186 _____ 165

Subtract.

A.

531	840	621	742
– 268	– 379	– 483	– 156

B.

925	436	631	860
– 548	– 249	– 189	– 374

C.

334	552	771	966
– 159	– 263	– 496	– 378

On another piece of paper, write a subtraction problem with regrouping. The difference should be 162.

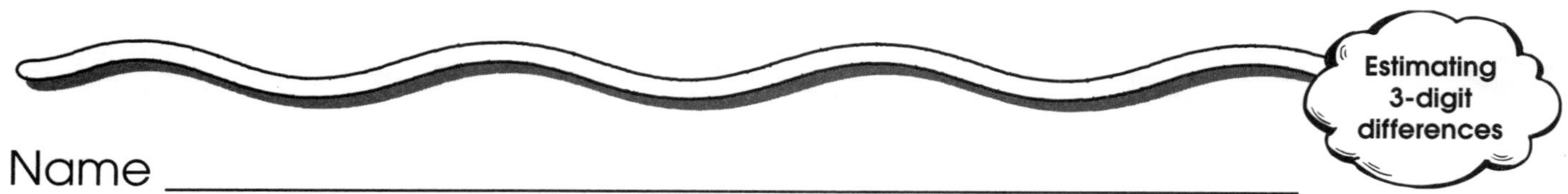

Name ______________________________

The Crowning Numbers

Prince Fritz cannot become king until he solves these subtraction problems. To help him, round each number to the nearest hundred and subtract. Then, find each real difference.

A. 637 → ☐
– 428 → – ☐

B. 527 → ☐
– 293 → – ☐

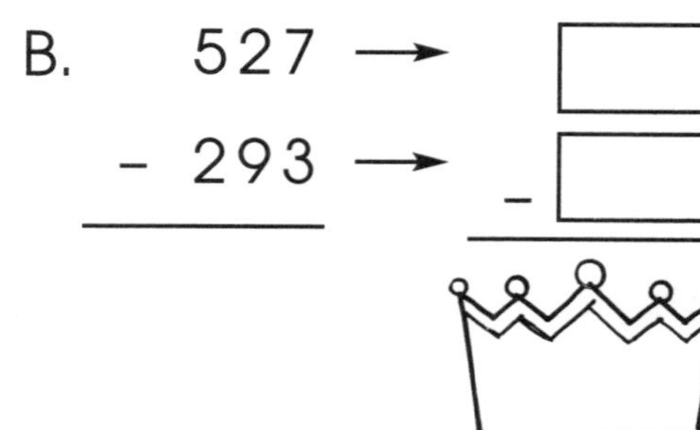

C. 724 → ☐
– 355 → – ☐

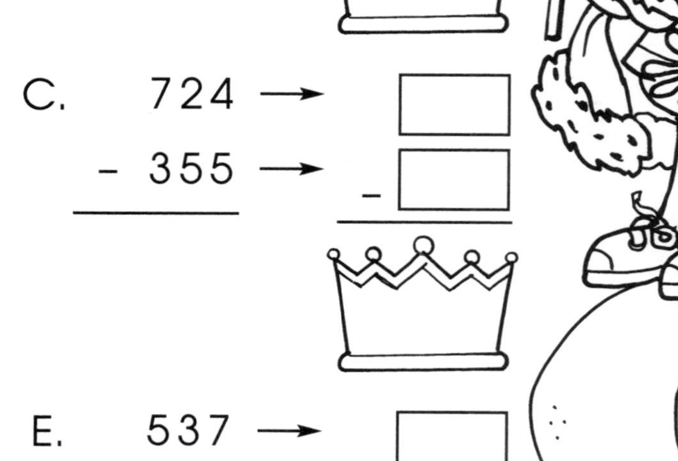

D. 935 → ☐
– 417 → – ☐

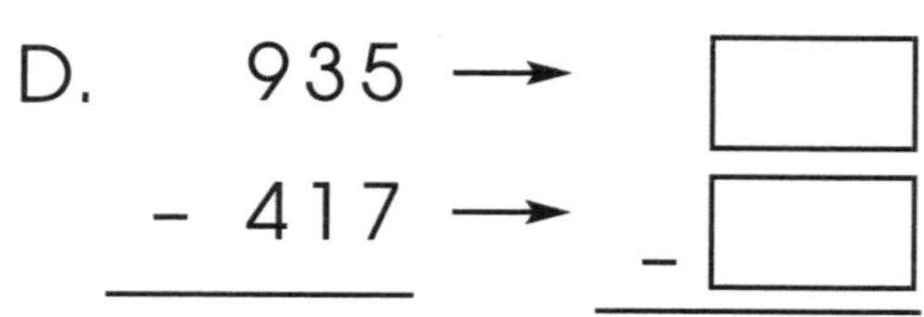

E. 537 → ☐
– 163 → – ☐

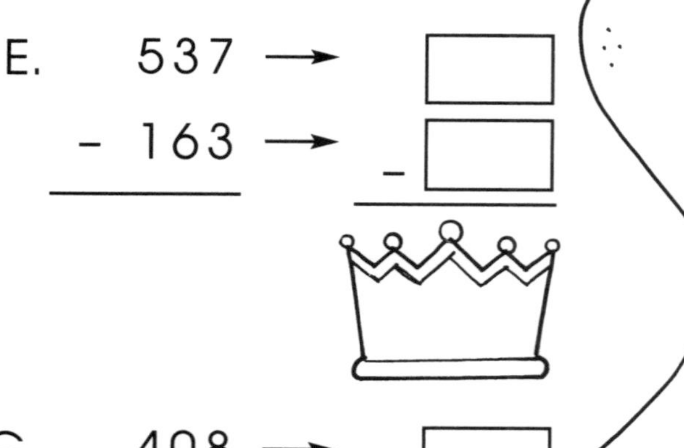

F. 814 → ☐
– 678 → – ☐

G. 408 → ☐
– 241 → – ☐

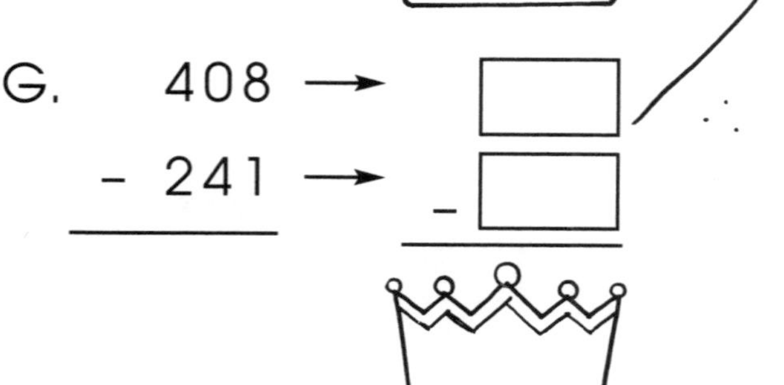

H. 713 → ☐
– 568 → – ☐

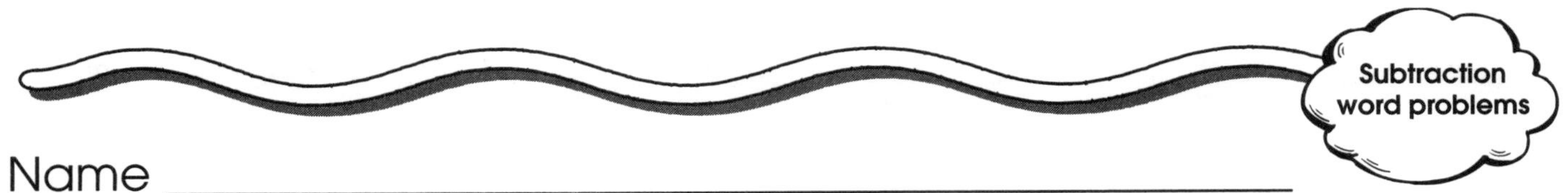

Name ____________________

Forest Figures

Solve each problem about the rain forest. Be sure to include the story unit with your answer.

A. One tree is 250 feet tall. Another tree is 125 feet tall. How many more feet is the taller tree?

B. Last year, it rained 263 inches in the rain forest. This year, it has rained 127 inches. How many more inches did it rain last year?

C. There are 43 kinds of ants living in a tree. Then, 17 kinds of ants move away. How many kinds of ants are left?

D. One gorilla weighs 323 pounds. Another gorilla weighs 291 pounds. How many more pounds does the first gorilla weigh?

Frogs cannot make their own body heat. They soak up the heat from the air.

Name ______________________________

Read All About It

Look for key words that tell you to add or subtract. Solve.

A. Fran read 102 pages on Saturday. She read 87 pages on Sunday. How many more pages did Fran read on Saturday?	B. Carlos counted 96 books in his classroom. Troy counted 88 books. How many books did they count in all?
C. Jasmine read for 63 minutes in the morning. After lunch, she read for 72 minutes. Before she went to bed, she read for 48 minutes. How many minutes did Jasmine read altogether?	D. Molly bought a book with 315 pages. She has read 196 pages. How many pages does she have left?
E. Emma counted 238 words in her book. Andy counted 197 words in his book. How many more words are in Emma's book?	F. Grant has read 57 books from the library. Jason has read 125 books. How many books have they read in all?

Telling time to the hour

Name________________________________

Watch Out!

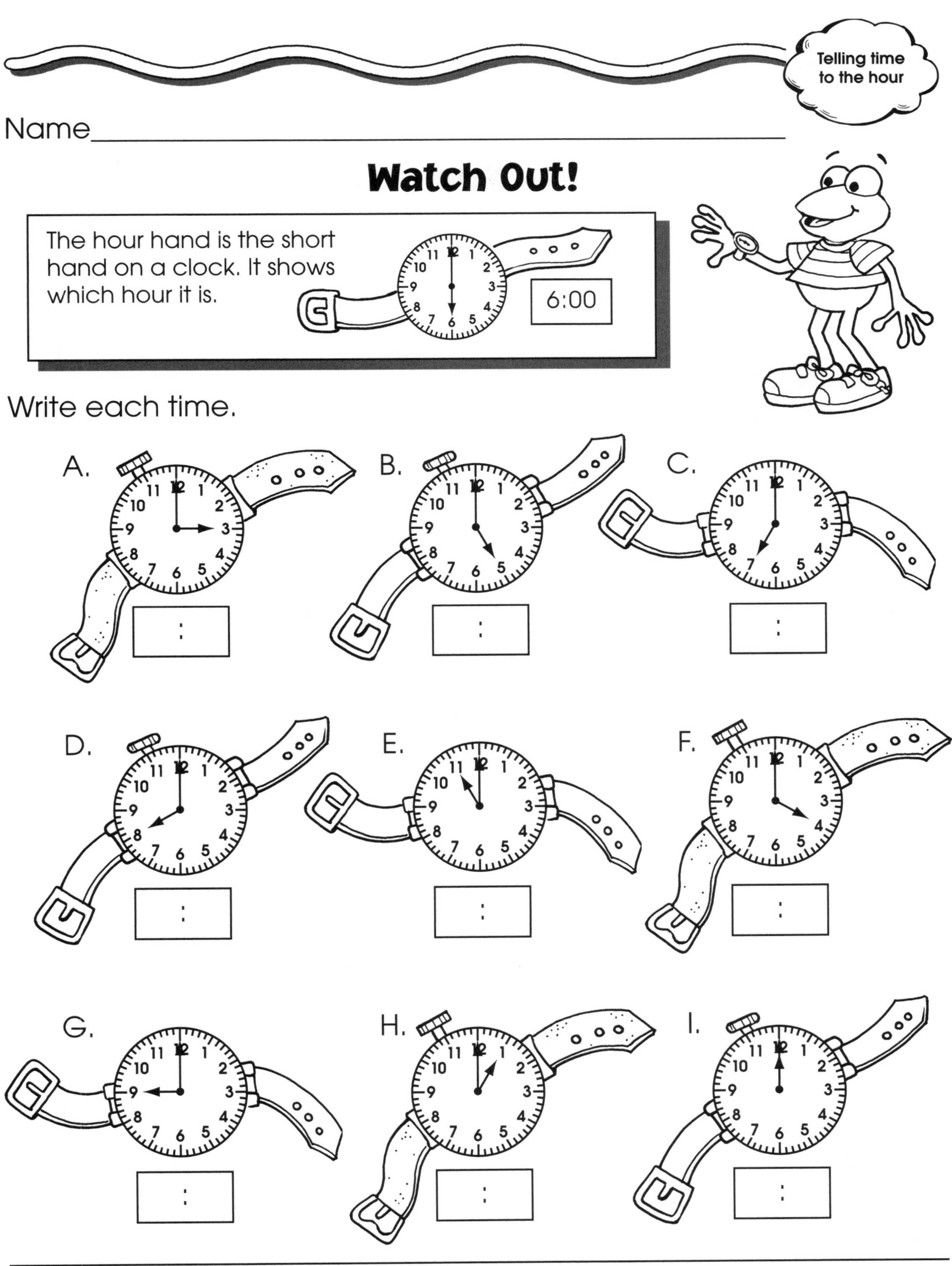

Name ______________________________

Track the Time

Look at the starting time. Then, look at the stopping time. Draw a line to the number of hours that have gone by.

Start **Stop**

A.

B.

C.

D.

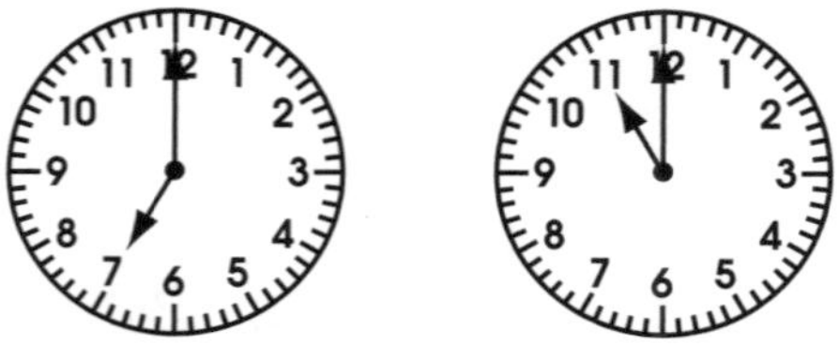

E.

Using time data from a table

Name ____________________

Off to Camp!

Use the table to complete each problem.

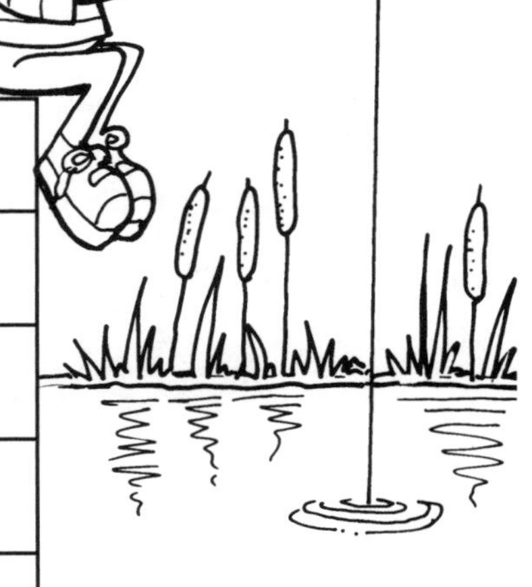

Riverside Camp Schedule

Activity	Start	End
hiking	8:00	10:00
archery	10:00	11:00
swimming	1:00	4:00
fishing	4:00	6:00
crafts	7:00	8:00

A. How long does swimming last? ________ hours

B. Which activities last two hours? ____________________

____

C. Which activity lasts the same amount of time as archery?

____

D. Draw the starting and ending times of fishing on the clocks.

Start

End

Telling time to the half hour

Name ________________________________

Time to Shine

The minute hand is pointing to the 6, so the time is 3:30.

Draw the hands on each clock to show the time.

A. 6:00

B. 2:30

C. 8:30

D. 4:30

E. 6:30

F. 11:00

G. 5:30

H. 11:00

I. 12:30

Name ______________________________

Light the Way

To find the path, color the clocks yellow that show the correct time.

A. 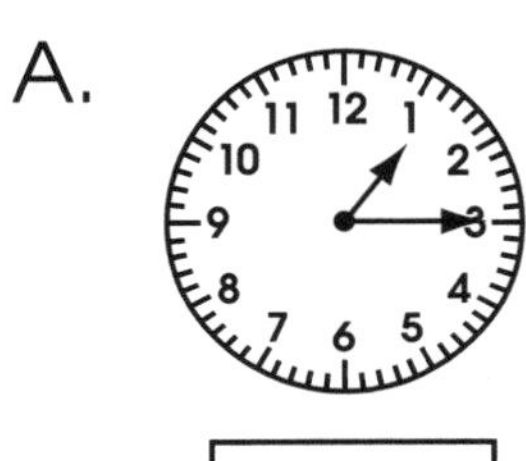 1:15

B.  3:25

C.  7:45

D.  9:50

E. 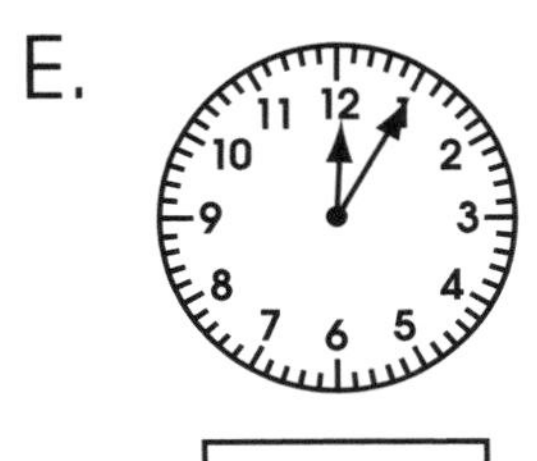 12:10

F.  8:35

G.   6:20

H.  10:30

I.  5:15

J.  2:40

K.  4:05

Estimating time

Name ______________________________

Minute by Minute

Estimate how long it would take to complete each activity. Circle your estimate.

A. Read a book. — less than a minute / more than a minute

B. Put on your shoes. — less than a minute / more than a minute

C. Write your name. — less than a minute / more than a minute

D. Paint a picture. — less than a minute / more than a minute

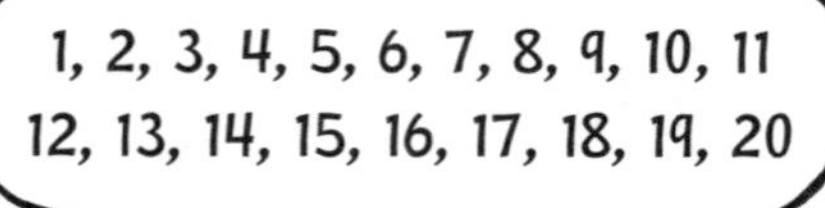

E. Count to 20. — less than a minute / more than a minute

Name two activities that take more than a minute.

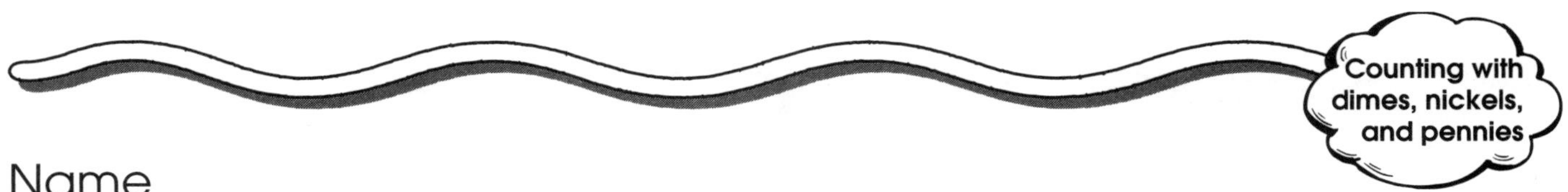

Name ____________________

Money Tree

Write the value of the coins on each tree.

A. ______¢ ______¢ ______¢

B. ______¢ ______¢ ______¢

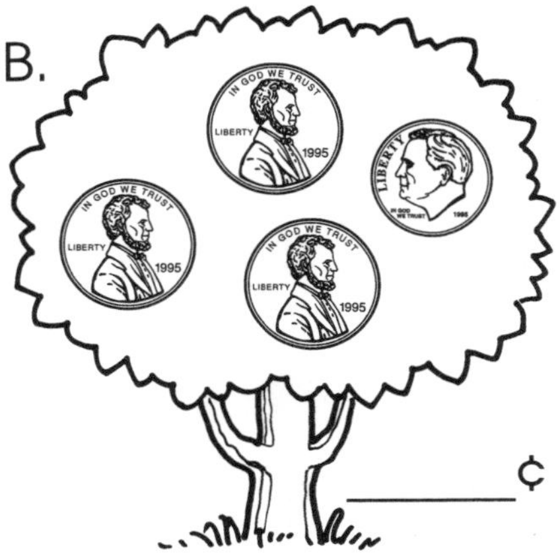

C. ______¢ ______¢

Draw coins to show 21¢.

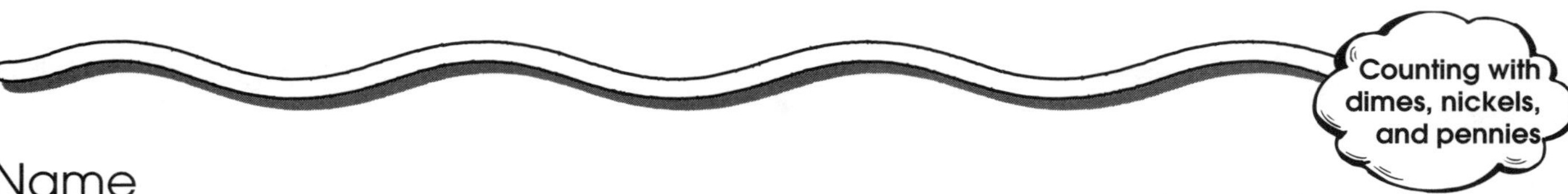

Name ____

Bake Sale

Circle the coins needed to buy each item.

A.

28¢

B.

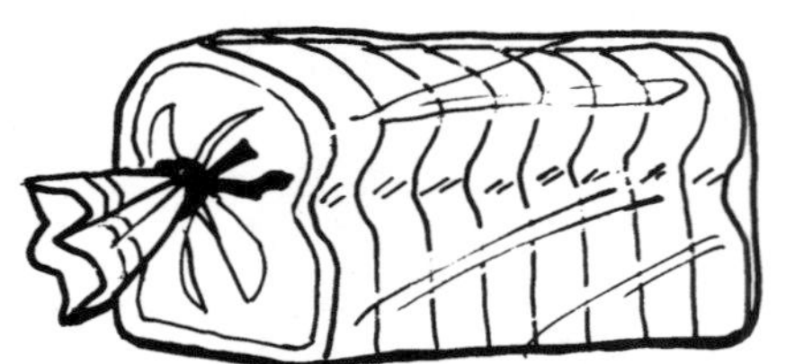

31¢

C.

15¢

D.

38¢

E.

23¢

Counting with quarters, dimes, nickels, and pennies

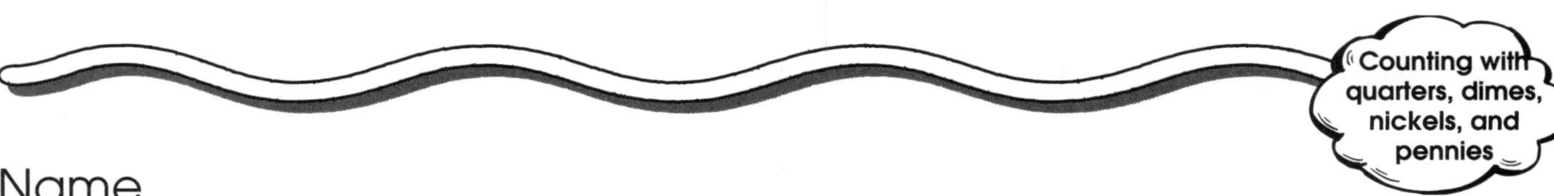

Name ____

Moneybags

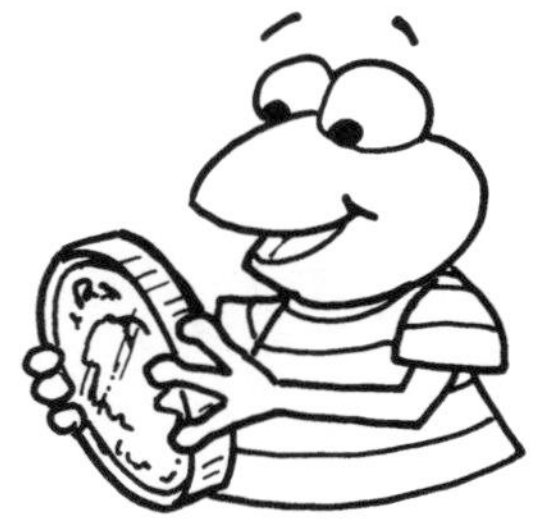

When counting money, start with the quarters.
Then, count the dimes, nickels, and pennies.

Color the bags with 25¢ blue. Color the bags with 36¢ yellow.
Color the bags with 51¢ red.

A.

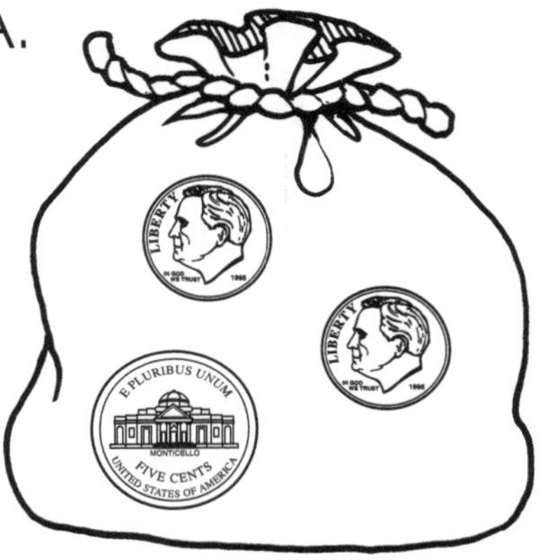

B.

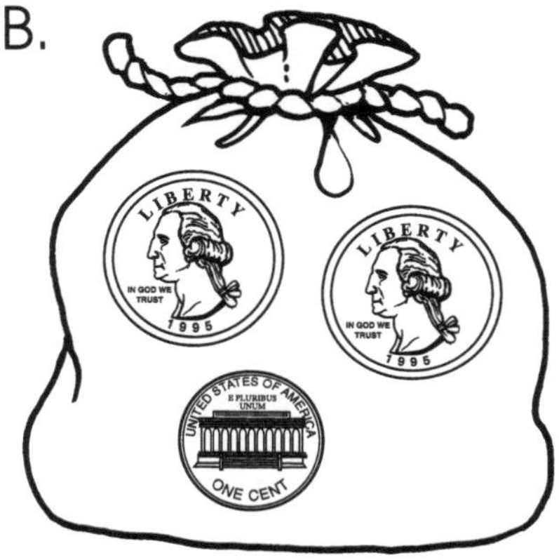

C.

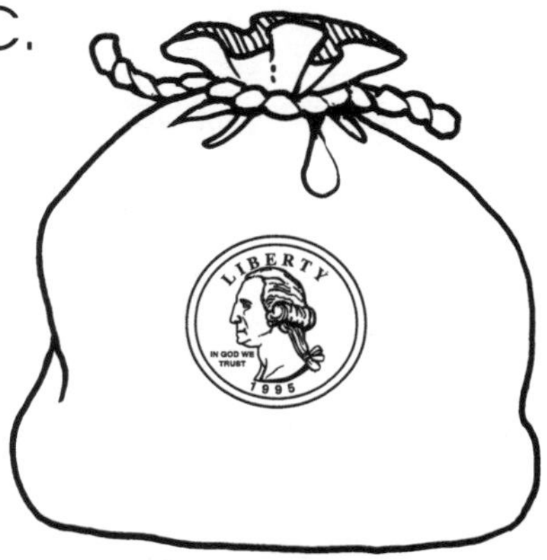

D.

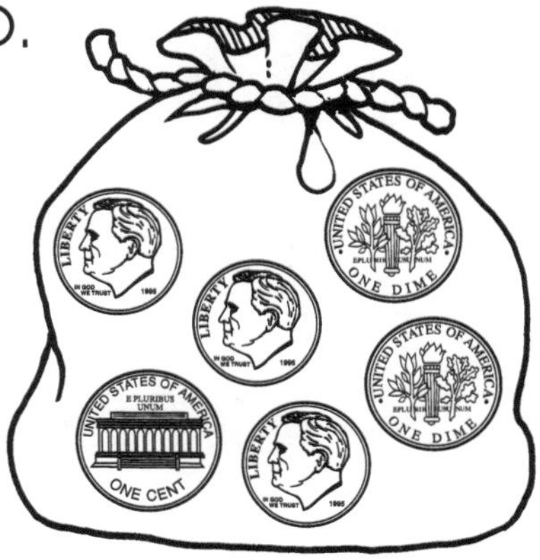

E.

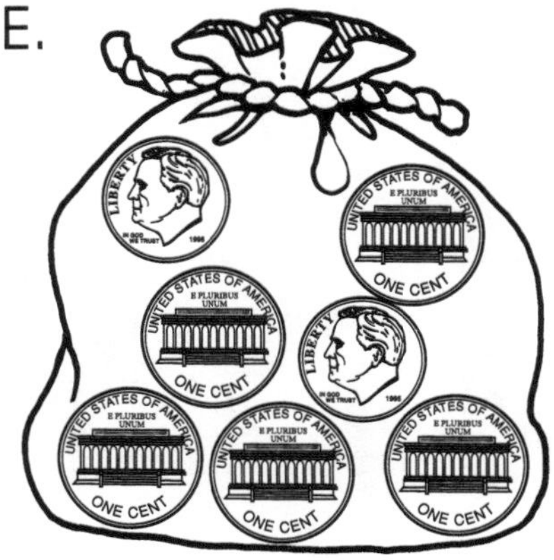

F.

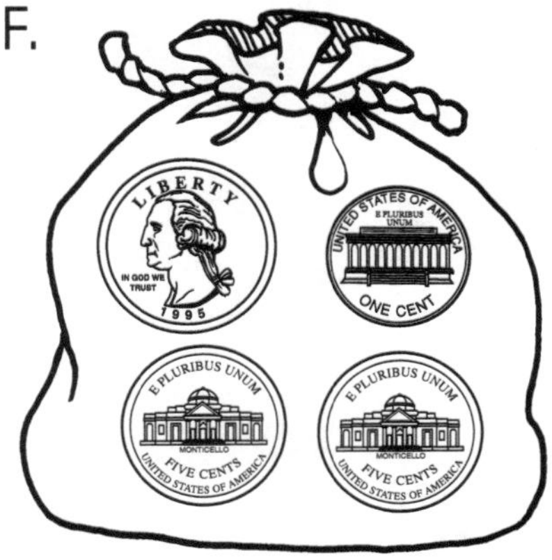

G.

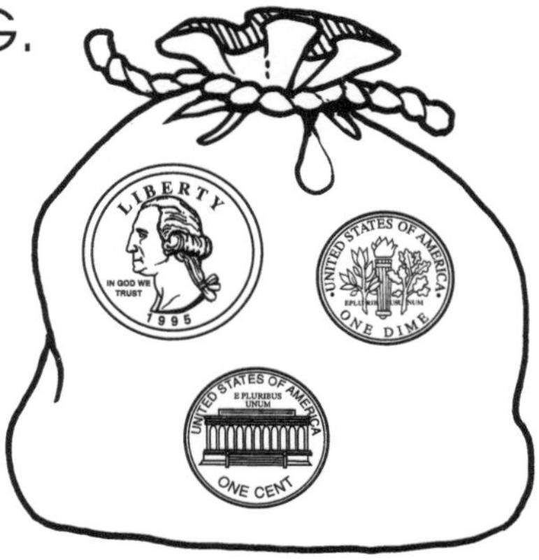

H.

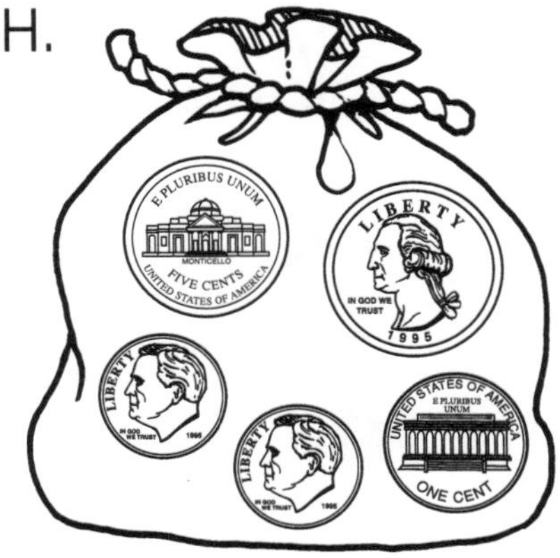

I.

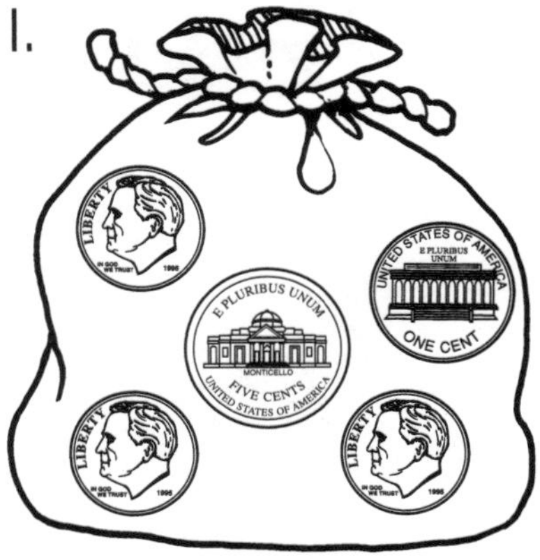

Name ______________________________

Change It Up

This is a half-dollar. It is worth 50¢.

Count the coins. Write the total on each notebook. Then, draw coins to show another way to make the total.

A.

B.

C.

D.

Name ______________________________

Dollar and Cents

One dollar is written $1.00.
The dollar sign comes first.
The decimal point comes between the dollars and cents.

Draw coins to show $1.00. Write how many.

A. Draw all half-dollars  .

There are _____ half-dollars in $1.00.

B. Draw all quarters  .

There are _____ quarters in $1.00.

C. Draw all dimes  .

There are _____ dimes in $1.00.

D. Draw all nickels  .

There are _____ nickels in $1.00.

Name ______________________________

Time to Shop

Circle **yes** or **no** to tell if  has enough money to buy each item.

A. 68¢ **yes** **no**

B. $1.30 **yes** **no**

C. 92¢ **yes** **no**

D. $2.15 **yes** **no**

E. 88¢ **yes** **no**

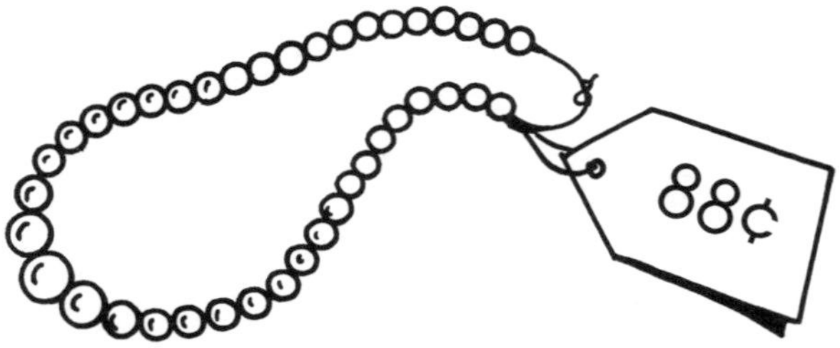

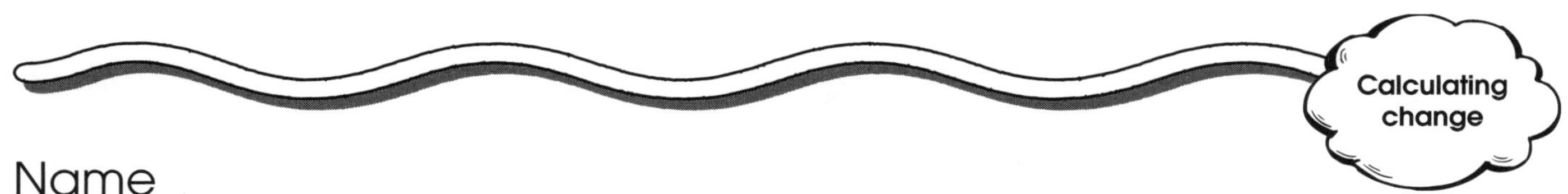

Name ______________________________

Place Your Order

To find out how much money you will get back when you buy something, make a subtraction problem.

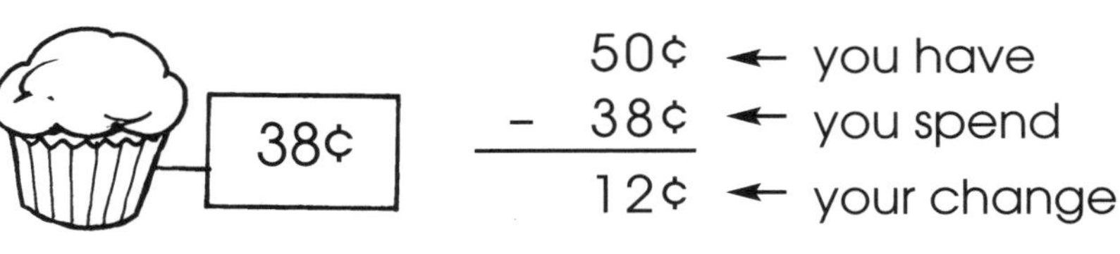

Write a subtraction problem to find out how much change you will receive.

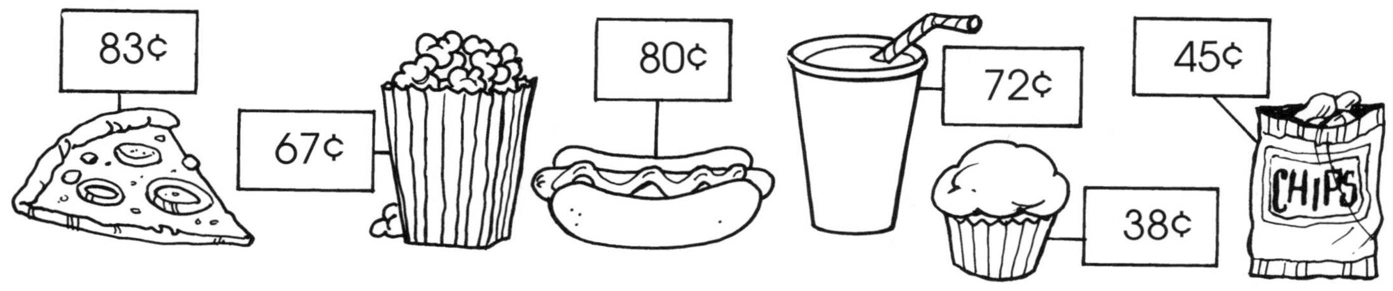

A.

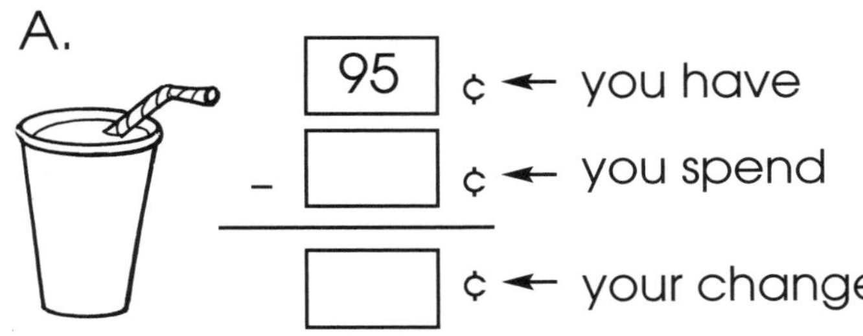

B.

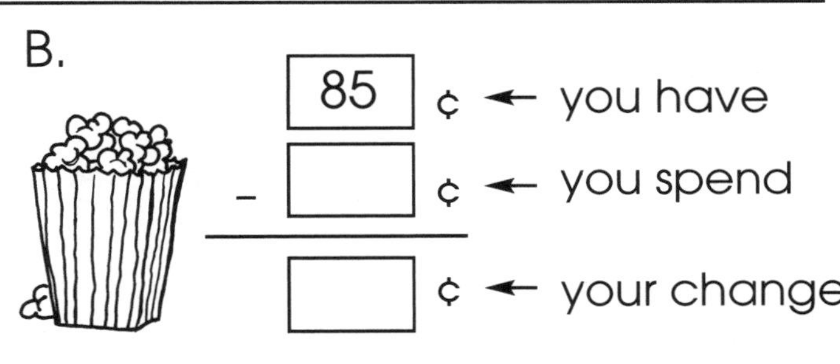

C.

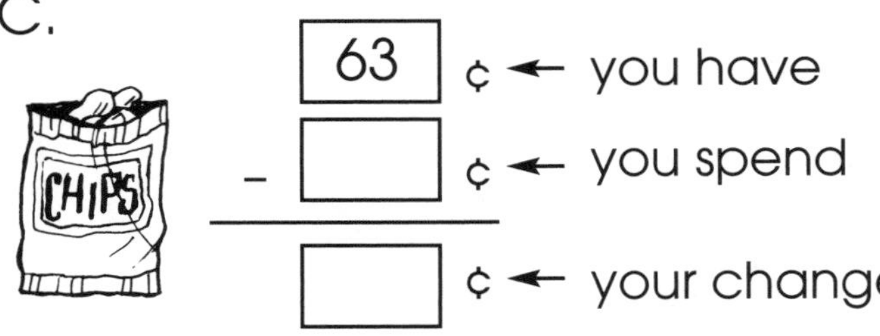

D.

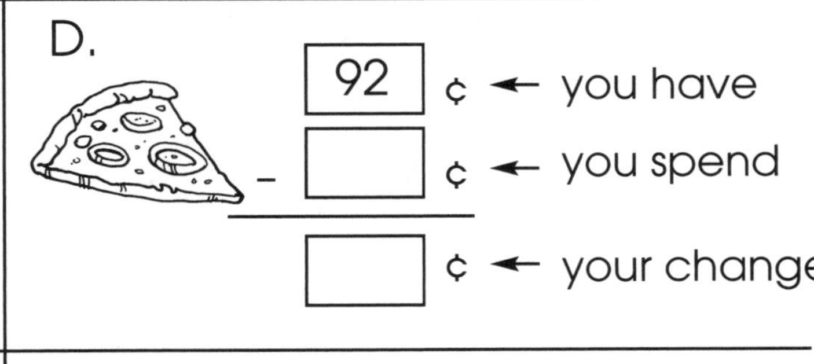

E.

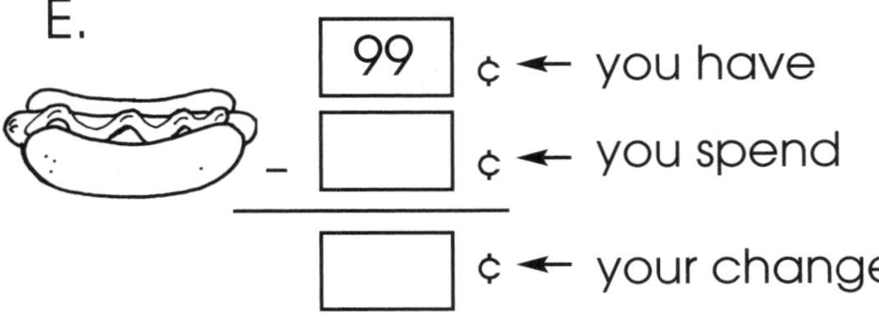

F.

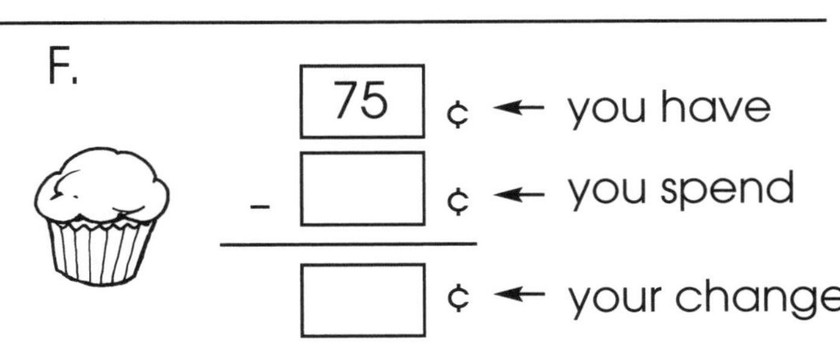

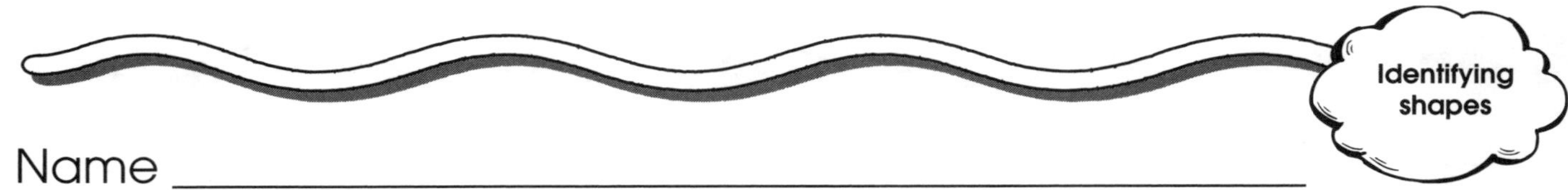

Name ____

Dancing Shapes

Count the number of each shape and write it in the shape chart. Then, write the name of the shape found the most to answer the riddle.

What is a math teacher's favorite kind of dancing?

__________________ dancing!

Shape Chart

shape	number
circle ○	____
square □	____
triangle △	____
rectangle ▯	____
oval ⬯	____

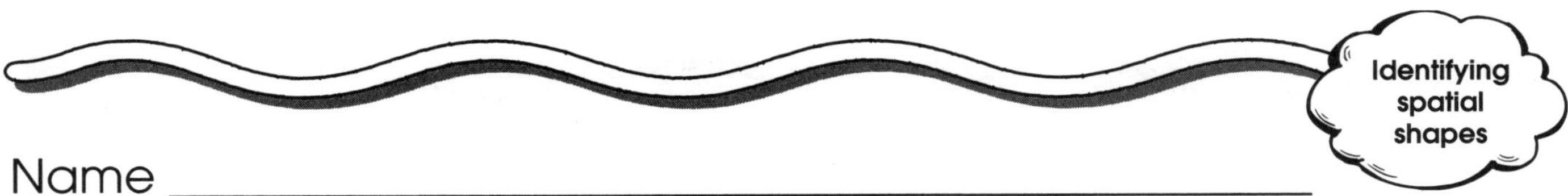

Identifying spatial shapes

Name ____

What's for Lunch?

These are **spatial shapes**.

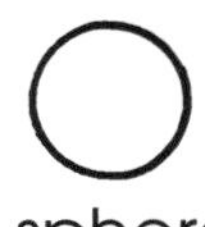
sphere

cube

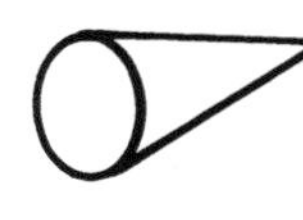
cone

rectangular prism

cylinder

Write the name of the spatial shape next to each food item.

A. 

____

B.  ____________________

C.  ____________________

D.  ____________________

E.  ____________________

F.  ____________________

G. 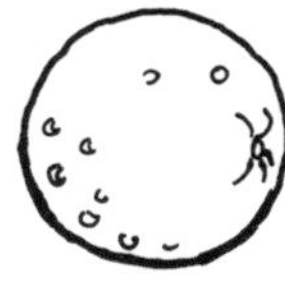 ____________________

H. 

____

What did you have for lunch? On another piece of paper, list each food and its spatial shape.

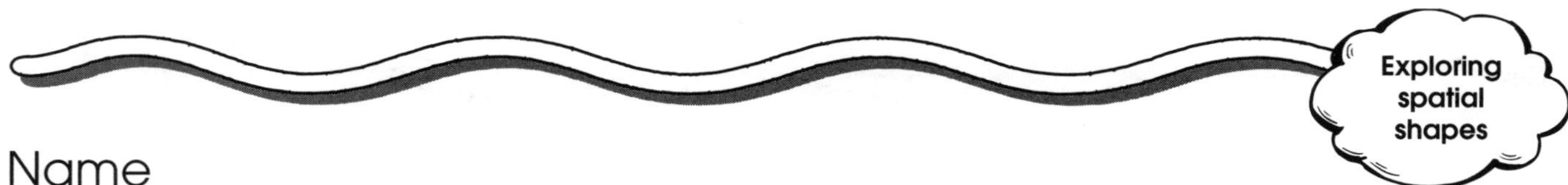

Name ______________________________

Face of a Shape

The flat side of a spatial shape is called a **face**.

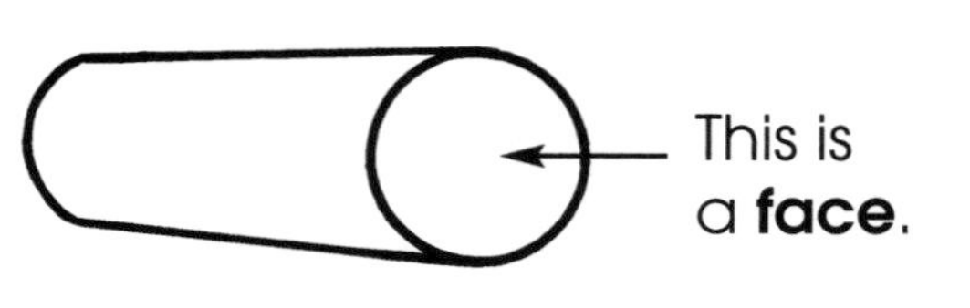

Complete the table.

spatial shape	number of faces

On another piece of paper, list 10 things shaped like a rectangular prism.

Identifying congruent shapes

Name ____________________

Just Alike

Congruent shapes are the same size and shape.

Color the shapes that are the same size and shape in each box.

A.

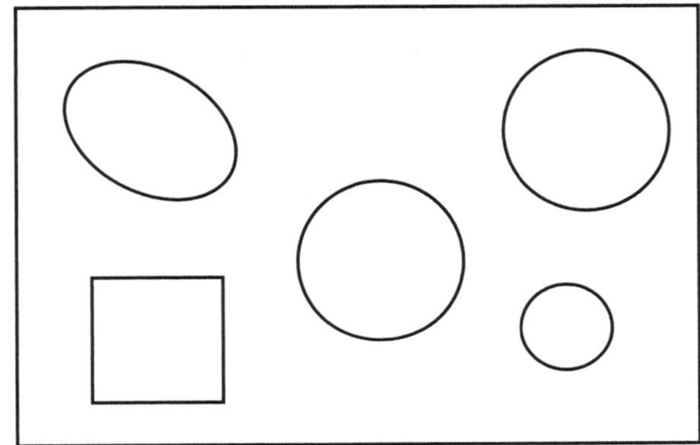

B.

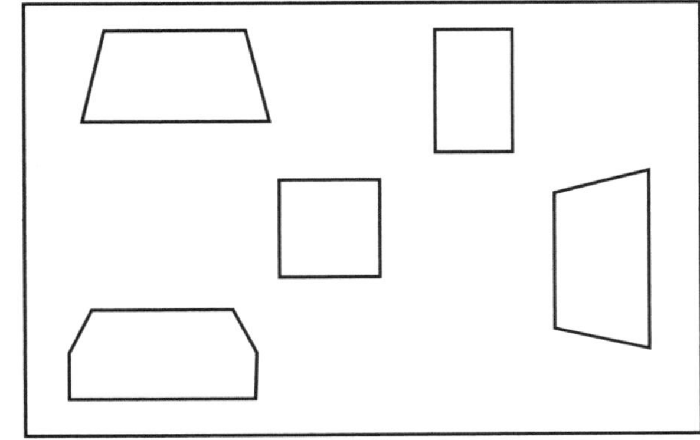

C.

D.

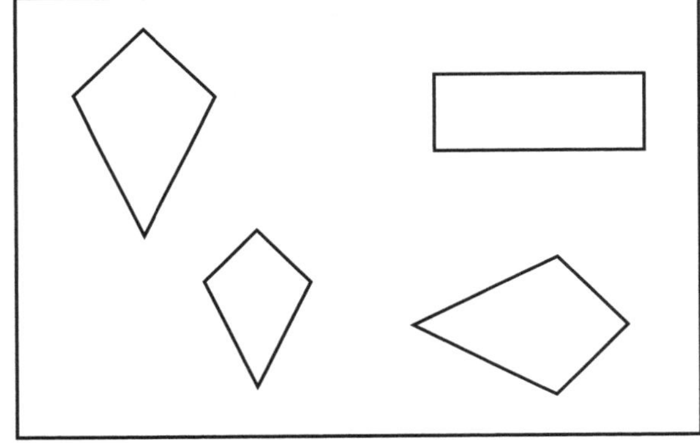

E.

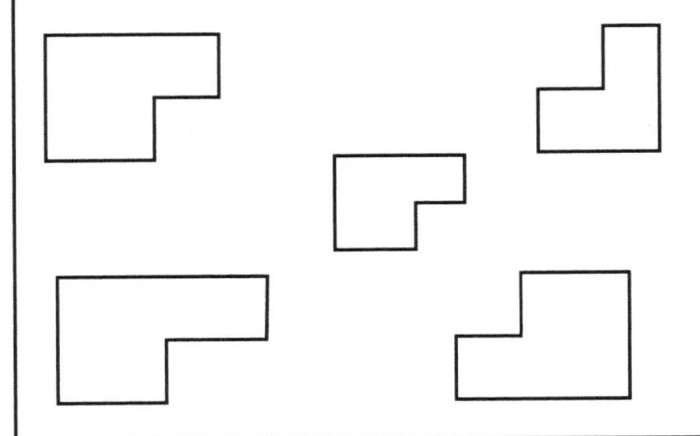

F.

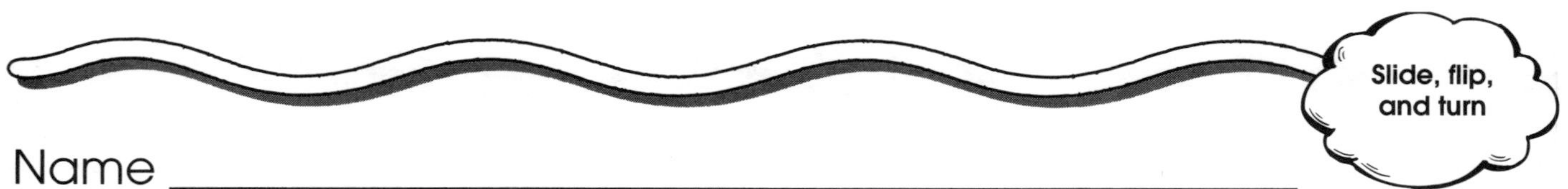

Name ______________________________

Moving All Around

slide flip turn

Circle how each shape is moved.

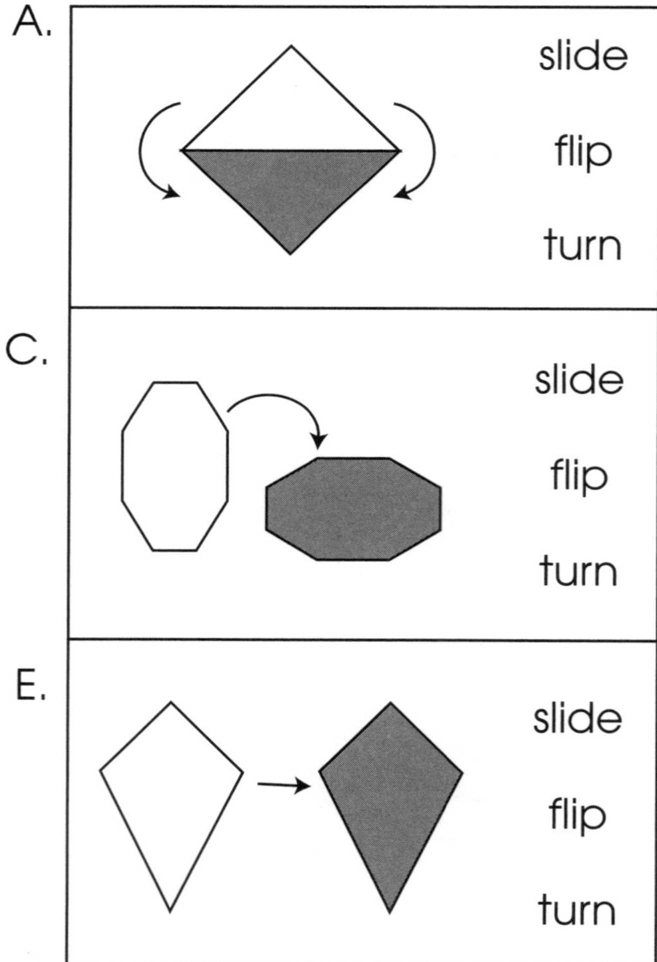

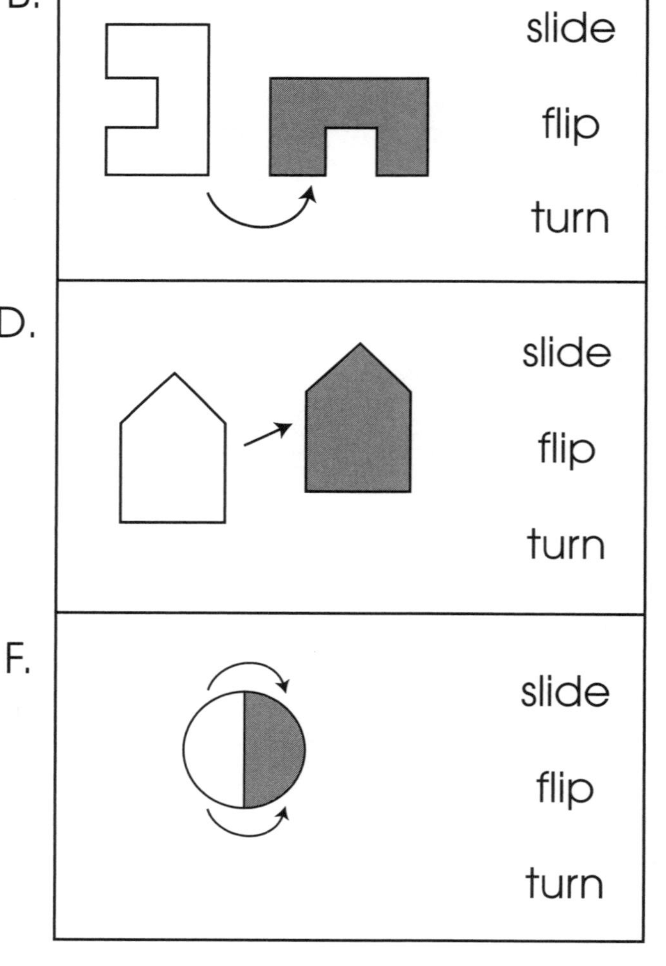

Exploring symmetry

Name ____

It's a Match!

Both sides of this shape are the same. It shows **symmetry**.

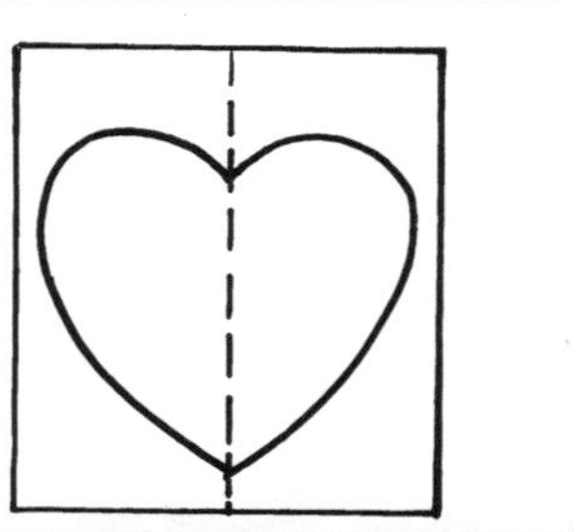

Draw the matching shape to show symmetry.

A.

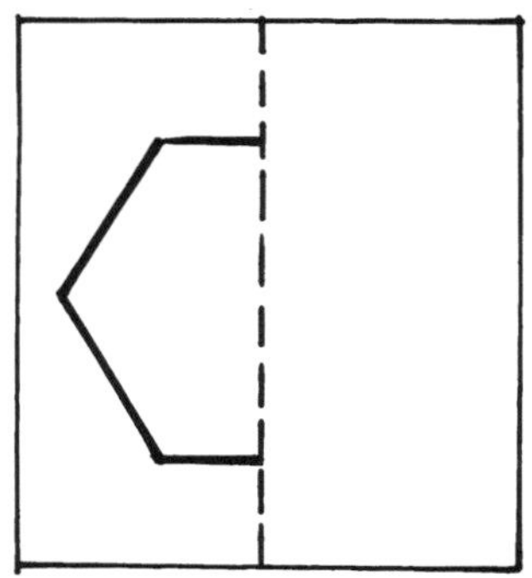

B.

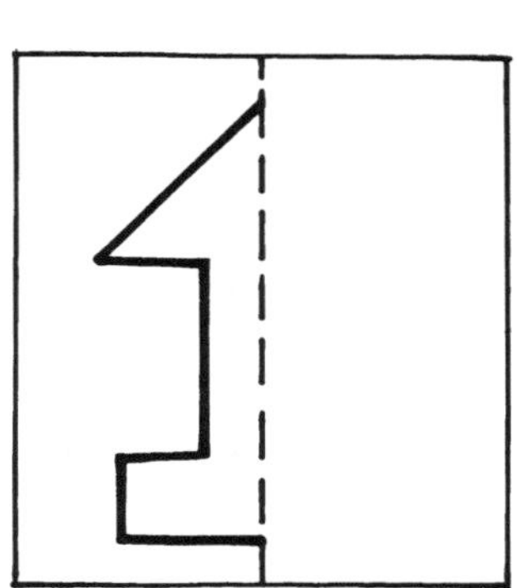

C.

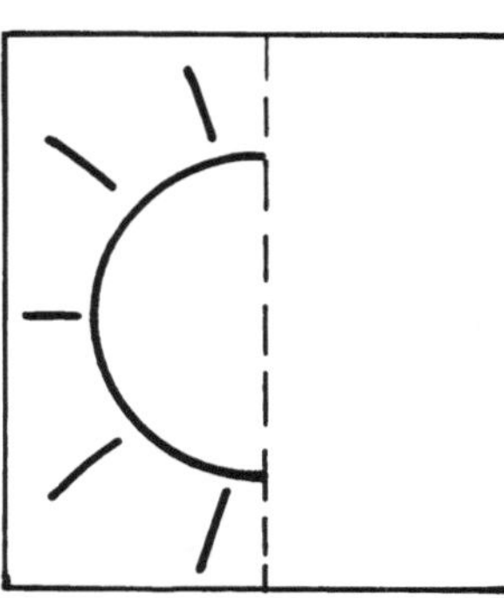

D.

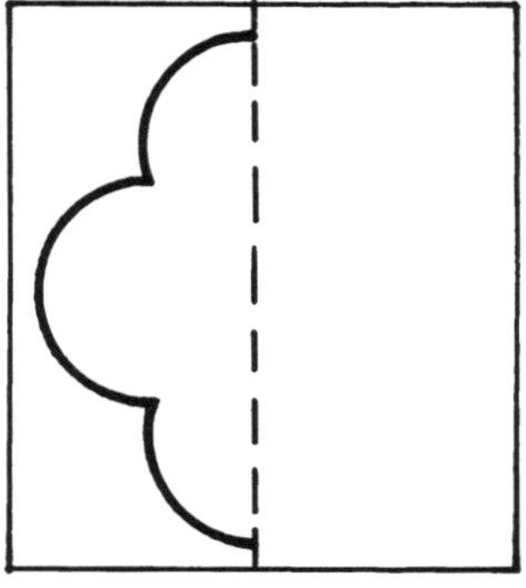

E.

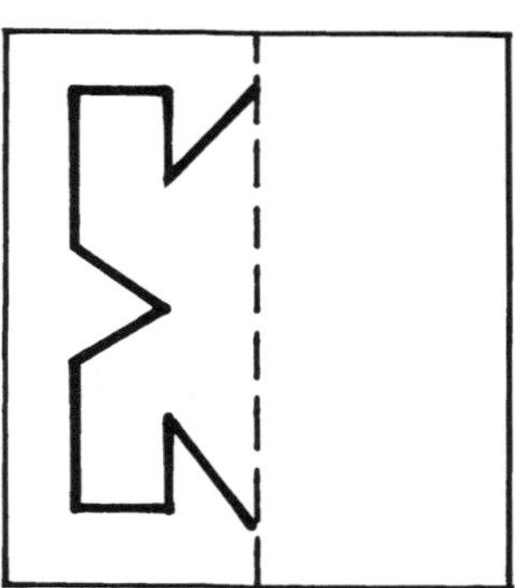

F.

G.

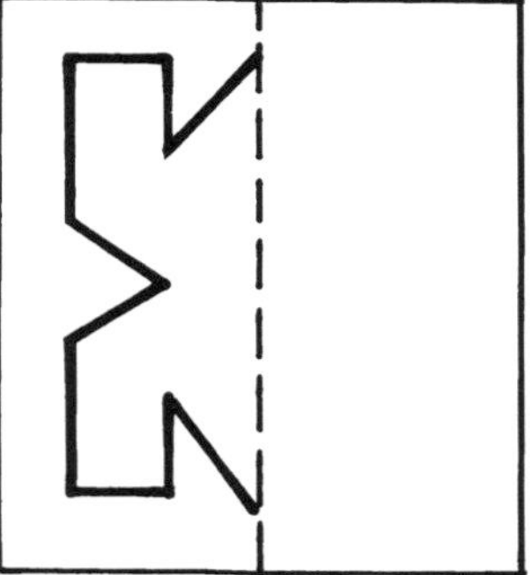

H.

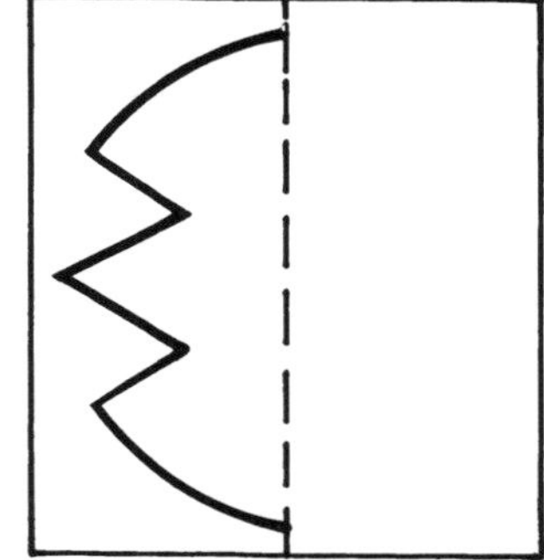

I.

Using logical reasoning

Name____

Choose the Cookie

Use the clues to find each cookie. Circle it.

A. I am the face of a cylinder.
My shape shows symmetry.

 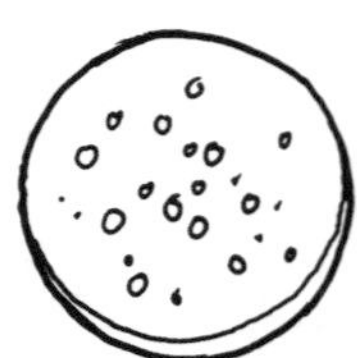 

B. I have four sides.
Each side is the same length.

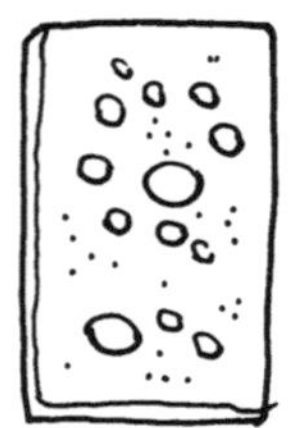 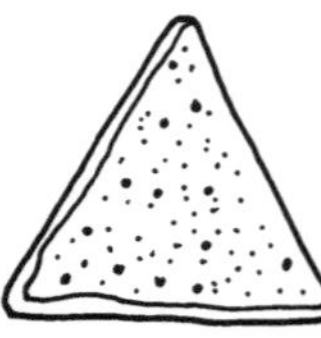  

C. I have three sides.
I am congruent to another cookie.
I have stripes.

D. My shape does not show symmetry.
I do not have stripes.

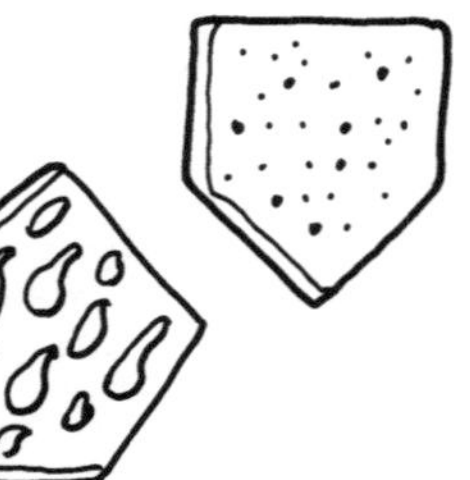 

E. I am not a square.
I am a face of a cone.

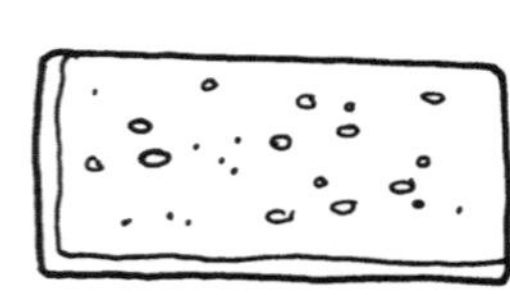   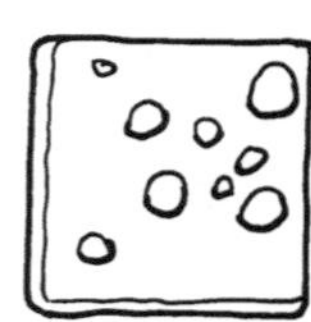

Name ____

Inching Along

Use a ruler to measure the length of each worm.

A.

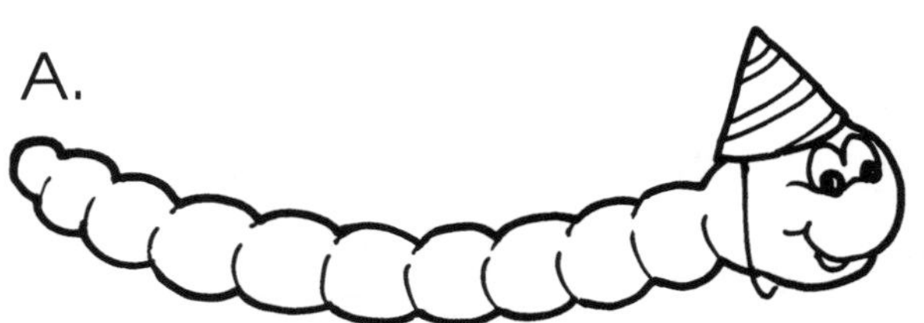

= ______ in.

B.

= ______ in.

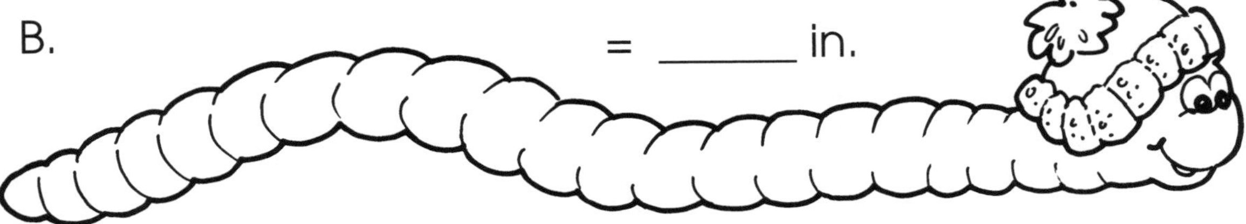

C.

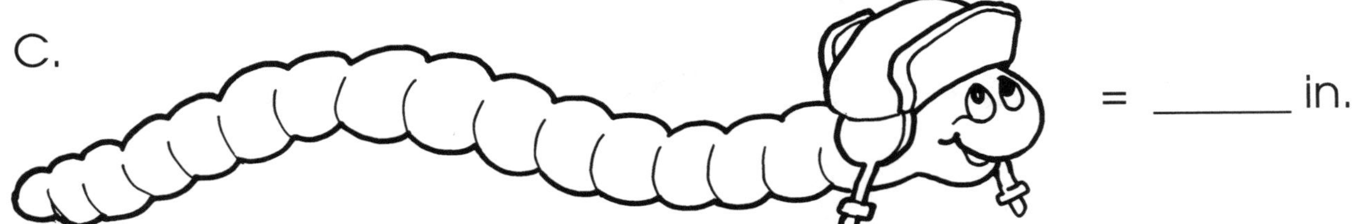

= ______ in.

D.

= ______ in.

E.

= ______ in.

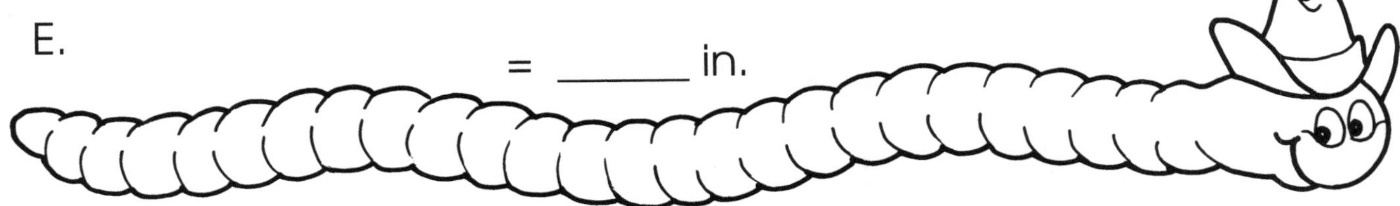

F.

= ______ in.

G.

= ______ in.

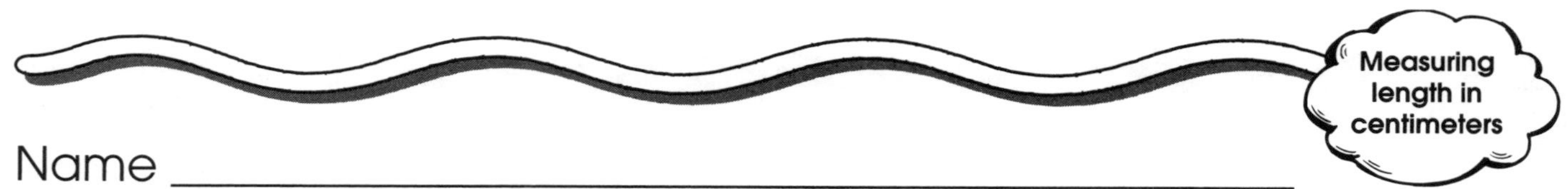

Name ________________________________

Doggy Fun

Use a ruler with centimeters to measure the line segments to each doghouse. Write the total distance. Then, use the code to answer the riddle below.

A. A ____ cm

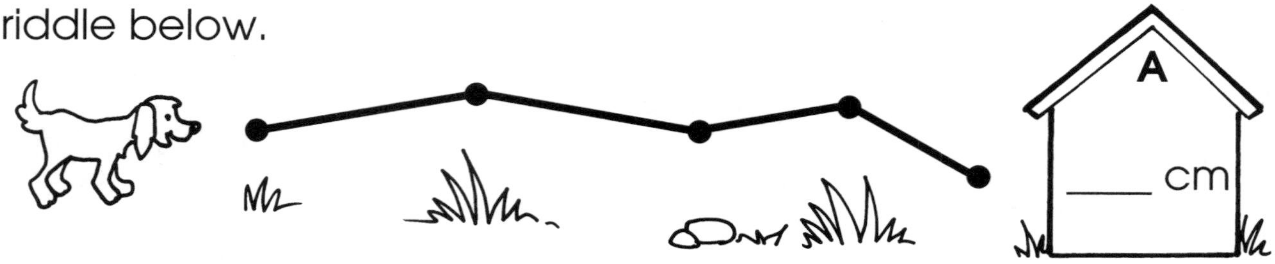

B. O ____ cm

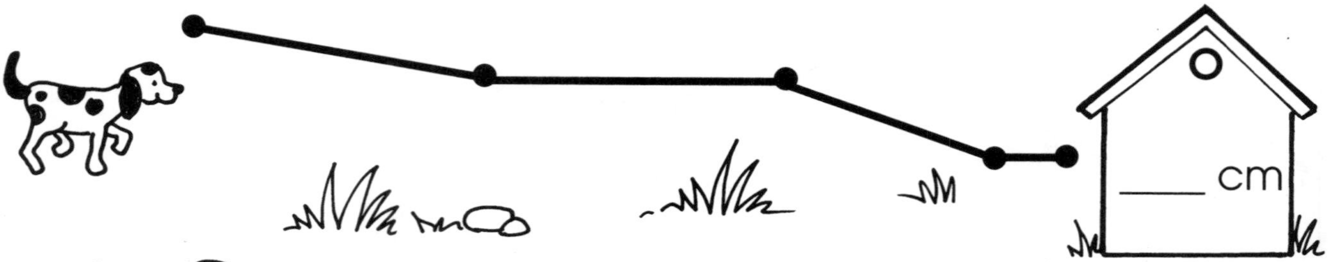

C. O ____ cm

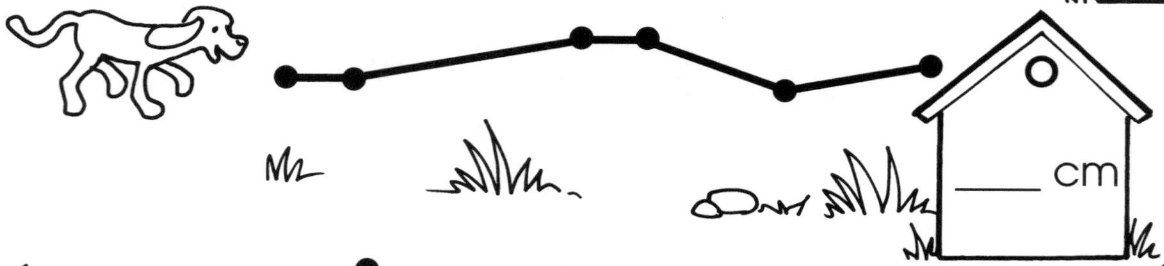

D. F ____ cm

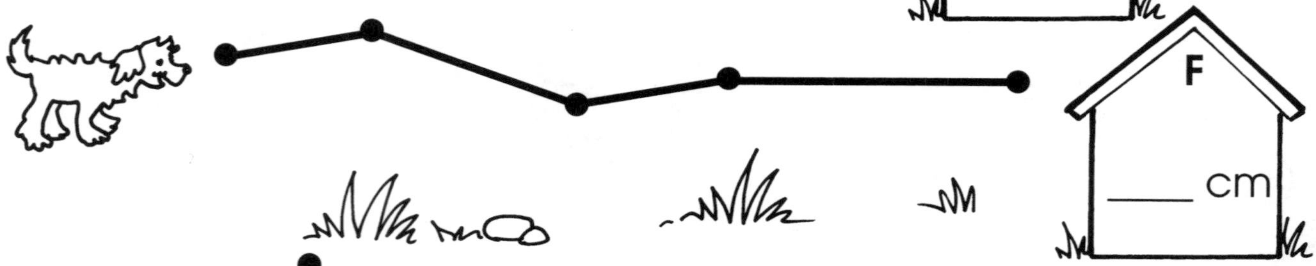

E. W ____ cm

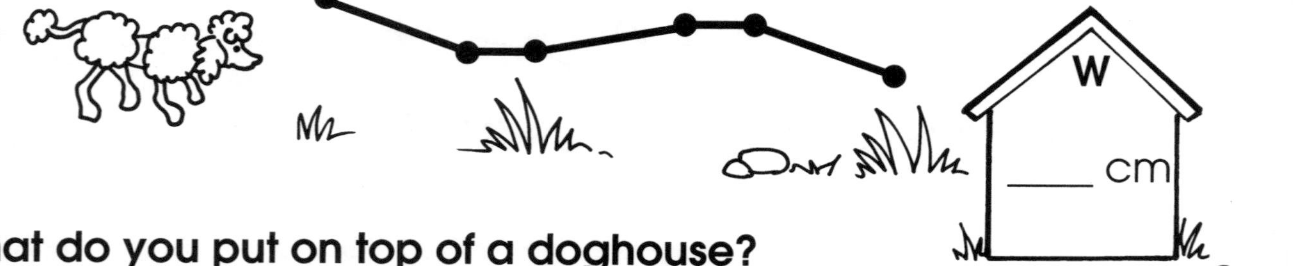

What do you put on top of a doghouse?

____ 10 ____ 8 ____ 12 ____ 9 ____ 11

DOG

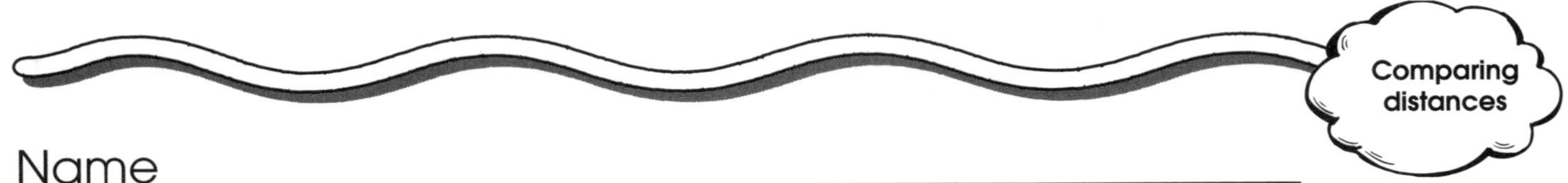

Name ____

Pencil Power

Tom's pencil is 4 inches long. Use the information below to complete the chart.

 Sam	____ in.
 Marie	____ in.
 Tom	4 in.
 Ning	____ in.
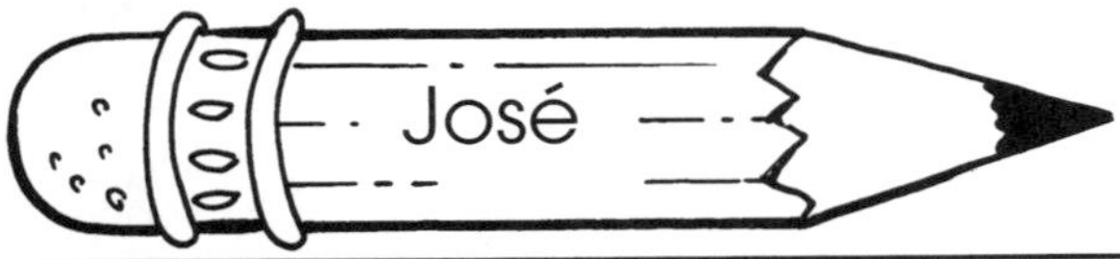 José	____ in.
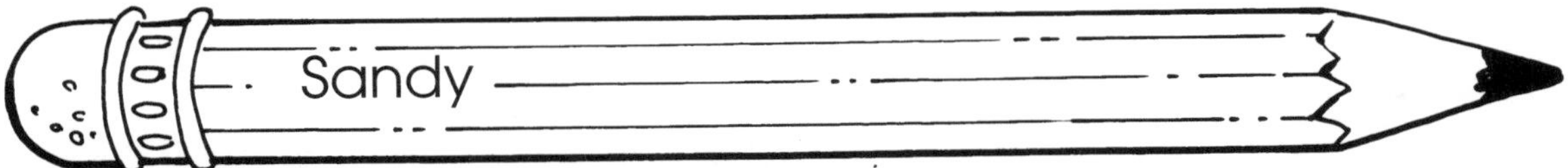 Sandy	____ in.

Marie's pencil is 1 inch longer than Tom's pencil.

José's pencil is 2 inches shorter than Marie's pencil.

Sandy's pencil is 3 inches longer than José's pencil.

Sam's pencil is 5 inches shorter than Sandy's pencil.

Ning's pencil is 1 inch longer than Sam's pencil.

Calculating the perimeter

Name ______________________________

Measure and Build

> The **perimeter** is the distance around something.
> To find the perimeter, add the length of each side.

It is time to build a new clubhouse. Find the perimeter for each board.

A.
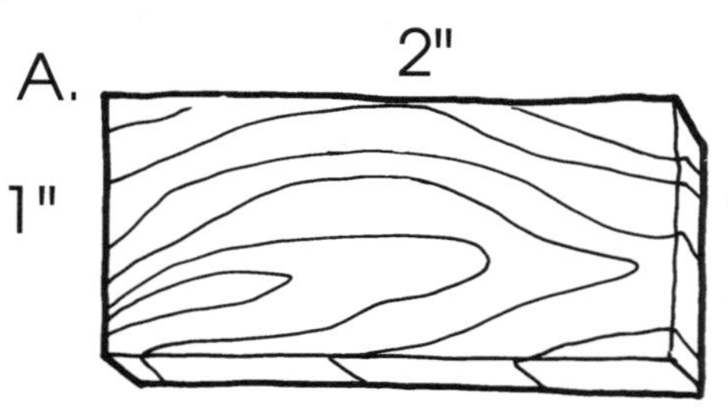

___ + ___ + ___ + ___ = ___ in.

B.

___ + ___ + ___ + ___ = ___ in.

C.

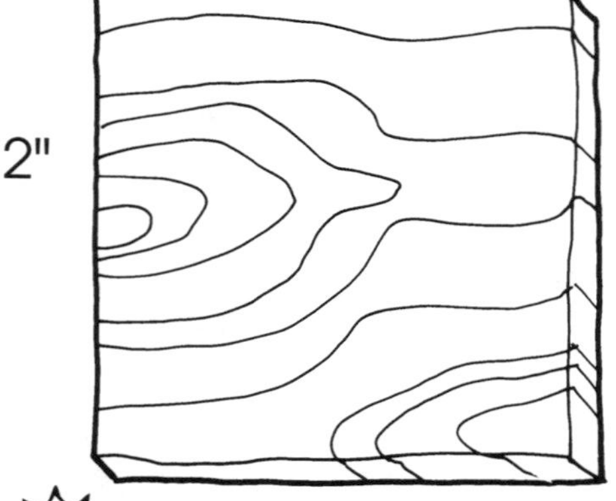

___ + ___ + ___ + ___ = ___ in.

Find a rectangle in your classroom. Find the perimeter.

Name ______________________________

A Pound of Fun

These things weigh about one pound.

Circle if each item is lighter or heavier than one pound.

A.

lighter than one pound | heavier than one pound

B.

lighter than one pound | heavier than one pound

C.

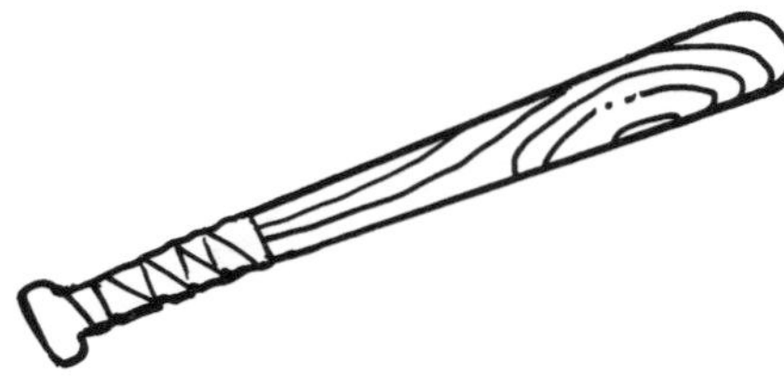

lighter than one pound | heavier than one pound

D.

lighter than one pound | heavier than one pound

E.

lighter than one pound | heavier than one pound

F.

lighter than one pound | heavier than one pound

Find three things heavier than a pound. Weigh each thing. Which is the heaviest?

Name ___________________________________

Guess the Weight!

A frog is lighter than one kilogram.

A big book weighs about one kilogram.

A dog is heavier than one kilogram.

Color the things that weigh less than one kilogram yellow.
Color the things that weigh more than one kilogram blue.

A kilogram is about two pounds. Find two objects that weigh less than a kilogram.

Comparing cups, pints, and quarts

Name ____________________

Measure Away

One way to measure liquids is with cups, pints, and quarts.

1 cup

2 cups = 1 pint

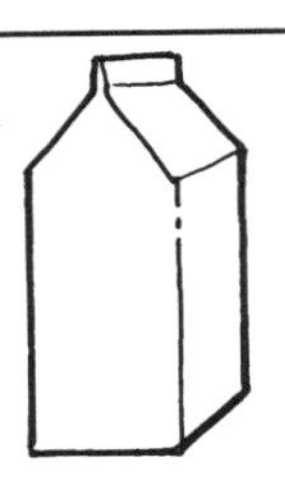

2 pints = 1 quart

Read each story. Then, follow the directions.

A. Mara drank 1 pint of orange juice. Color the number of cups she drank.

B. Mr. Chow bought 2 quarts of milk at the store. Color the number of pints he bought.

C. Spot drank 2 pints of water. Color the number of quarts he drank.

D. Brad used 2 pints of water to make lemonade. Color the number of cups he used.

E. Mrs. Roberts bought 1 quart of orange juice and 1 pint of apple juice. Color the number of pints of juice she bought in all.

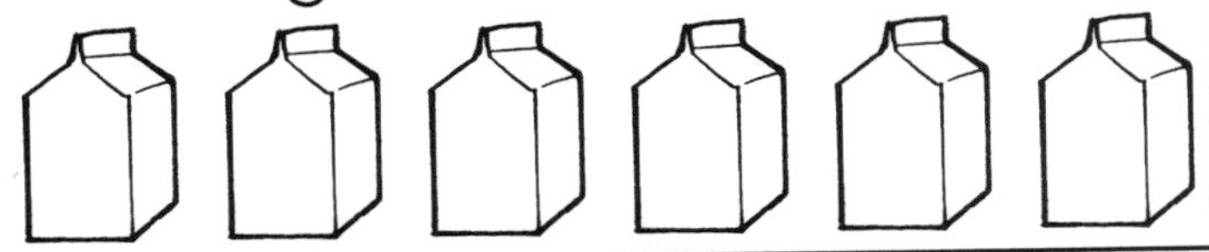

F. There are 4 pints of milk in the refrigerator. Color the number of quarts of milk.

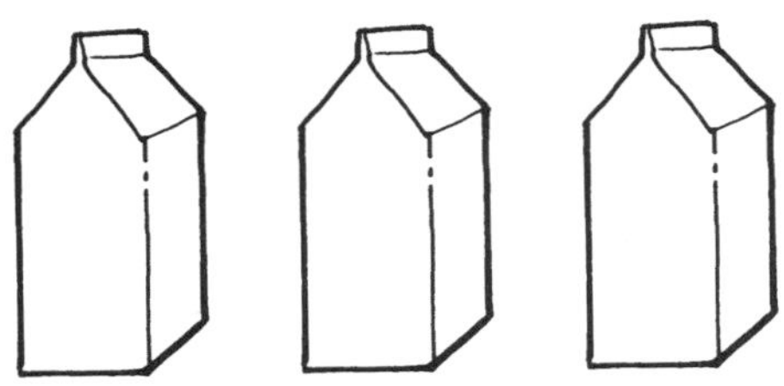

Name ____________________

A Liter of Liquid

A liter is another way to measure liquids.

Circle the container that holds only about 1 liter.

A.

B.

C.

D.

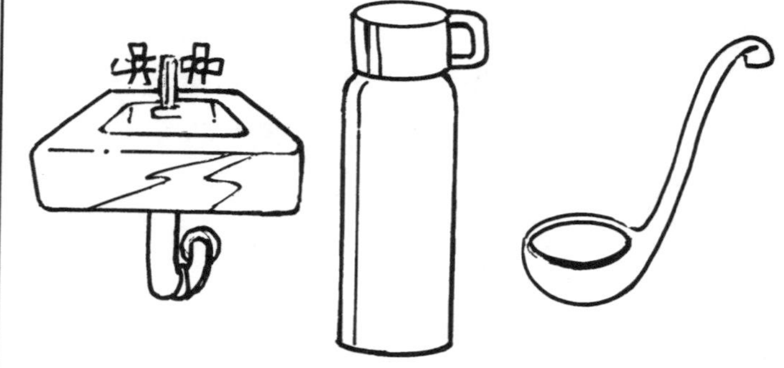

E.

F.

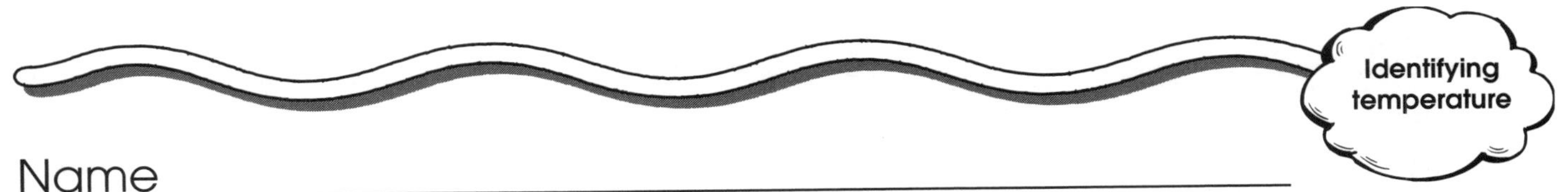

Name ____

What's the Temperature?

Circle the temperature for each picture.

A.

20° F 0° F 65° F

B.

15° F 50° F 90° F

C.

20° F 70° F 50° F

D.

5° F 45° F 75° F

On another piece of paper, list five activities you could do when it is 70° F.

Name ______________________________

Recess Fun

Mrs. Mason's class has earned an extra recess! They voted to decide what to do. Use the bar graph to answer each question below.

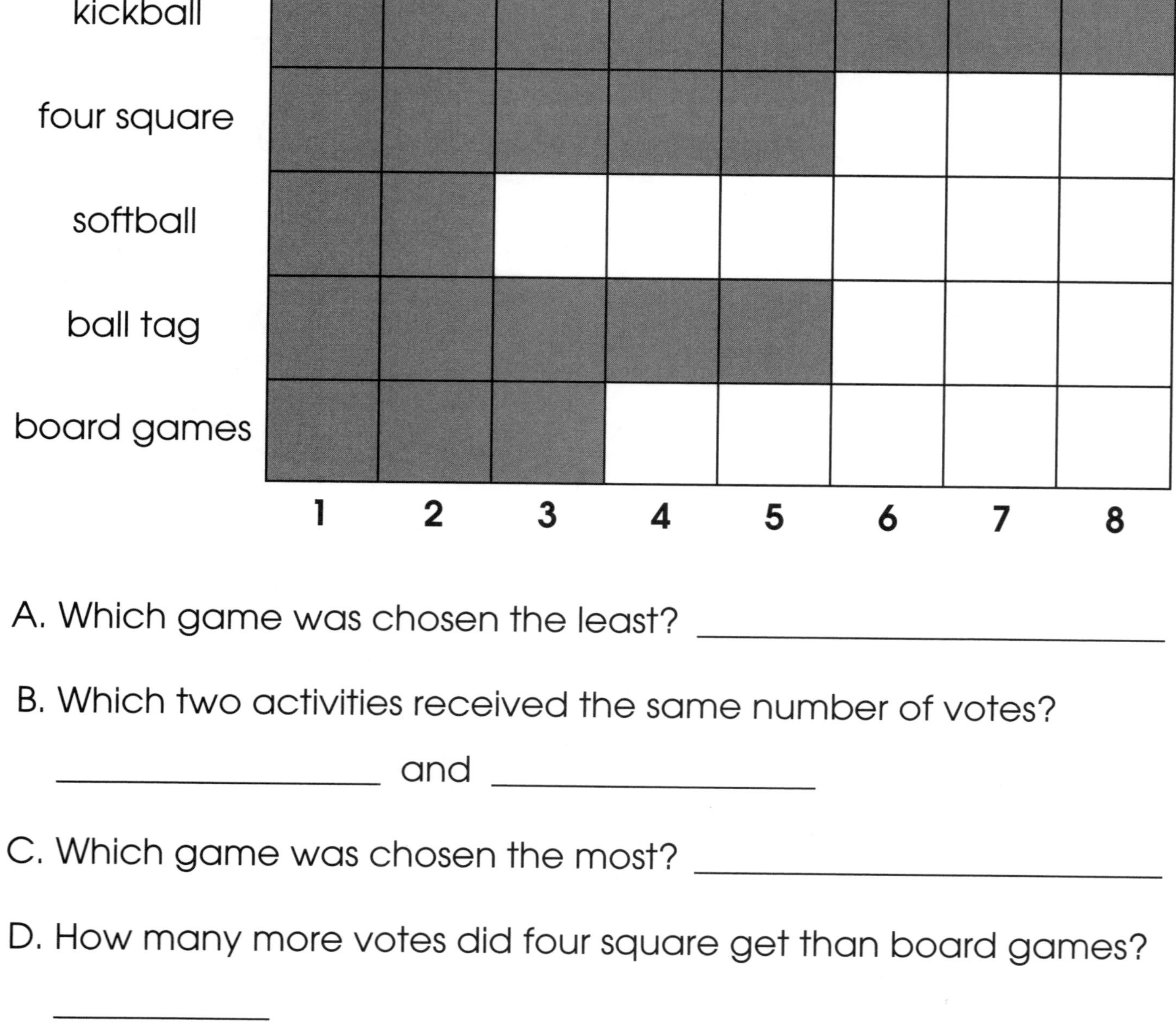

A. Which game was chosen the least? ______________

B. Which two activities received the same number of votes?

______________ and ______________

C. Which game was chosen the most? ______________

D. How many more votes did four square get than board games?

____

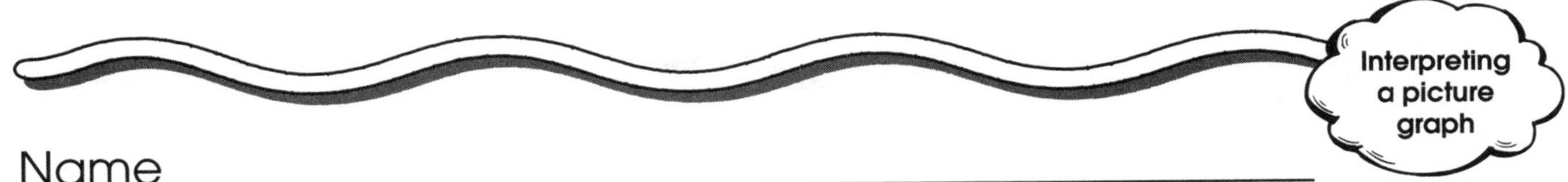

Name ______________________________

Shoot and Score

Use the picture graph to answer each question.

Team Goal Totals

Claire	⚽ ⚽ ⚽
Ming	⚽ ⚽ ⚽ ◐
Stan	⚽ ⚽ ⚽ ⚽ ⚽ ⚽
Sara	⚽ ⚽ ⚽ ⚽ ⚽ ⚽ ⚽
Carlos	⚽ ⚽ ◐
David	⚽ ⚽ ⚽ ⚽

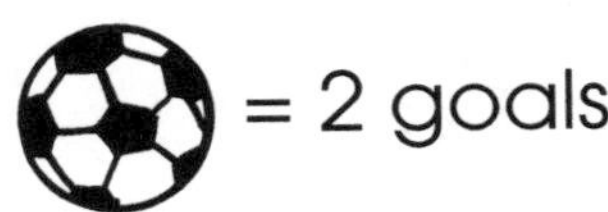

A. Who scored eight goals? ______________________

B. How many goals did Ming score? ______________________

C. Who scored the least number of goals? ______________________

D. How many goals did Stan and Sara score in all? ______________

E. How many more goals did Stan score than Claire? ______________

Often, 8-year-old soccer players use a soccer ball that is 24 inches around. Measure your soccer ball.

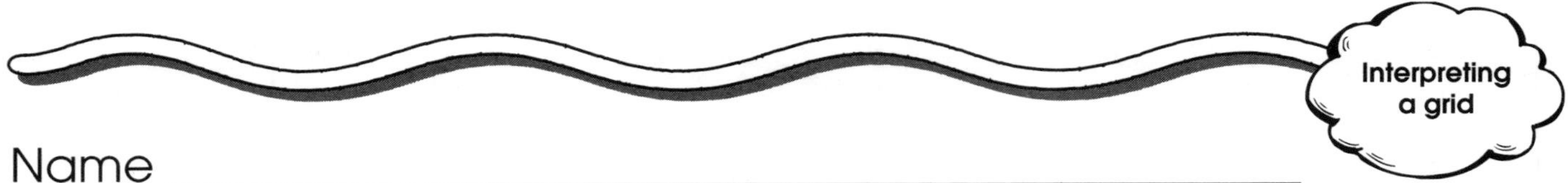

Name ____

Garden Grid

To read a grid, find the letter at the bottom. Then, go up to the number.

Name the vegetable that is found at each place on the grid.

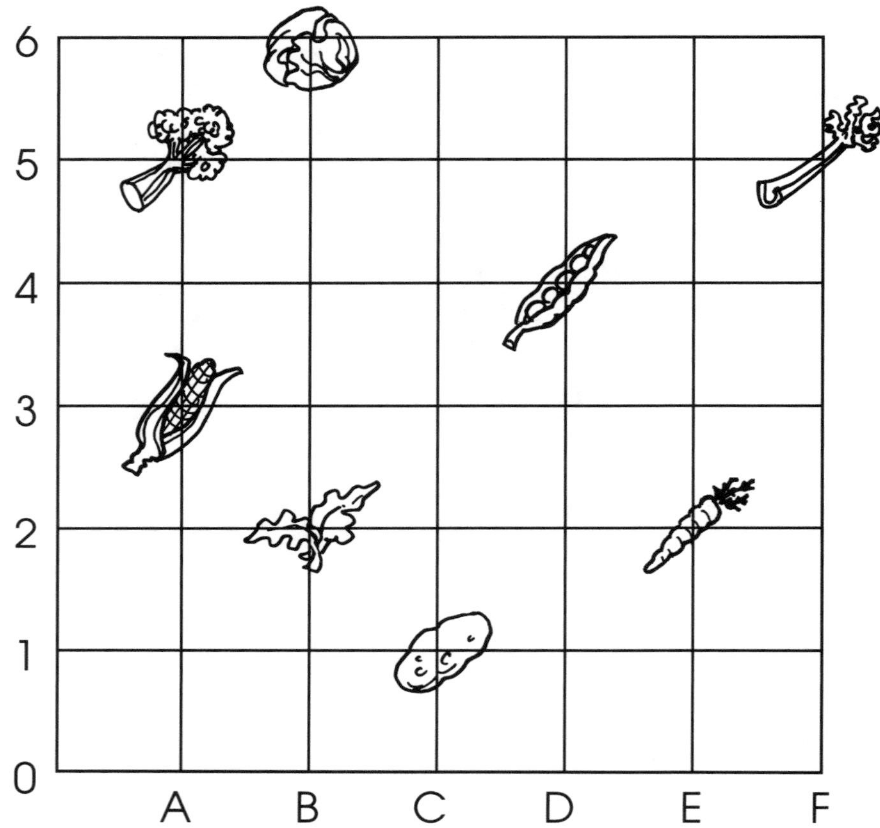

A. (C, 1) ____________________

B. (E, 2) ____________________

C. (F, 5) ____________________

D. (A, 5) ____________________

E. (B, 6) ____________________

F. (D, 4) ____________________

G. (A, 3) ____________________

H. (B, 2) ____________________

Name ______________________________

Colorful Shapes

Color the shapes with two equal parts blue. Color the shapes with three equal parts red. Color the shapes with four equal parts yellow. Do not color the shapes with unequal parts.

A. 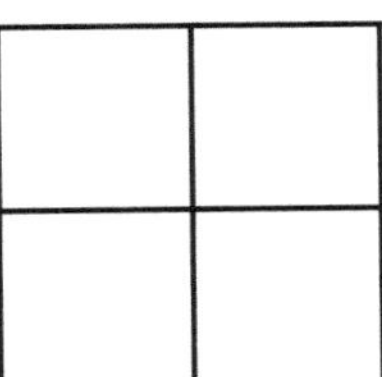

B. 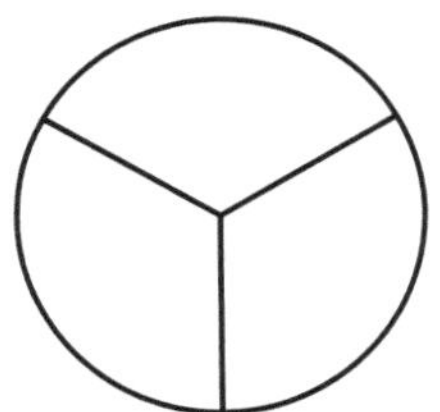

C. 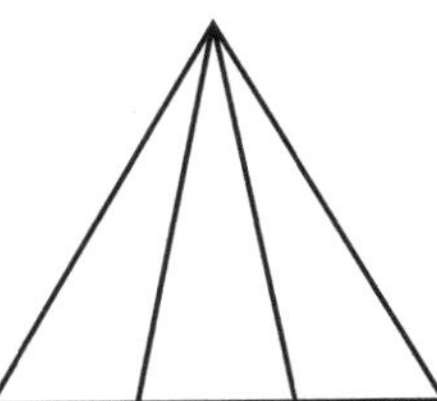

D. 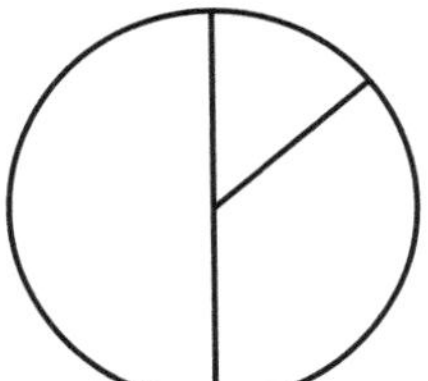

E. 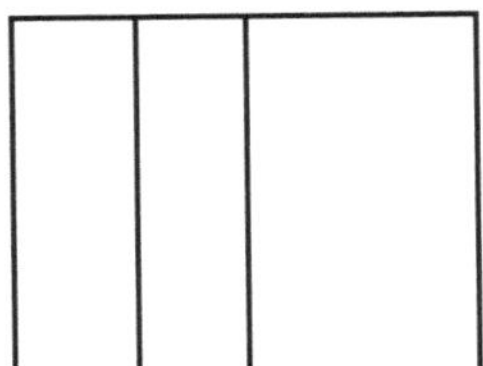

F. 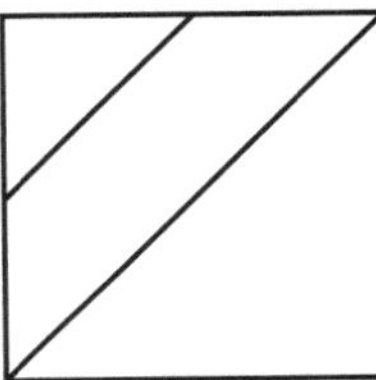

G. 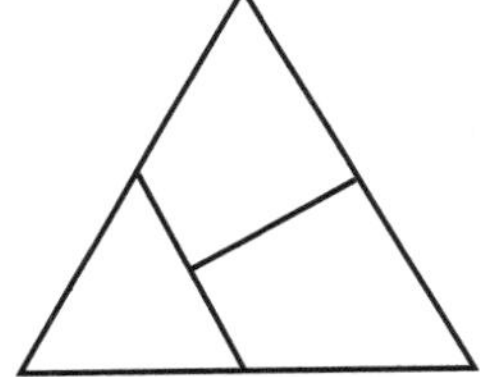

H. 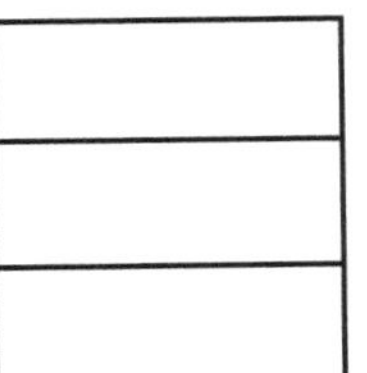

I. 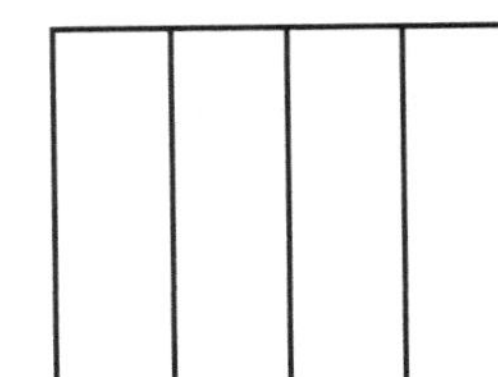

J. 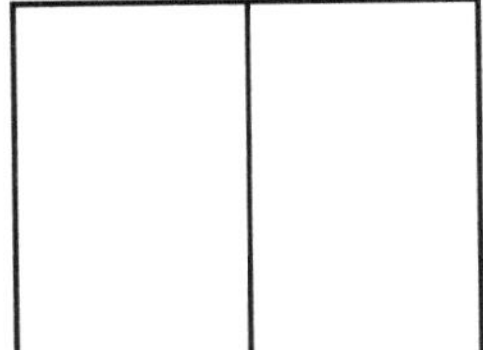

K. 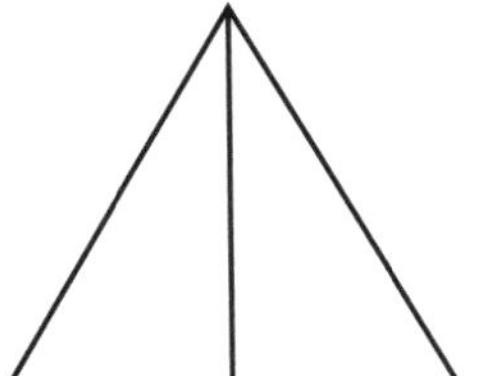

L. 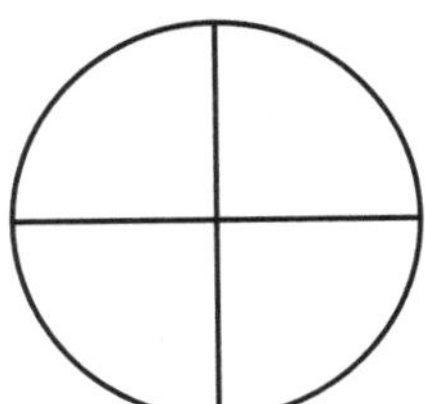

Show two different ways to divide a rectangle into 4 equal parts.

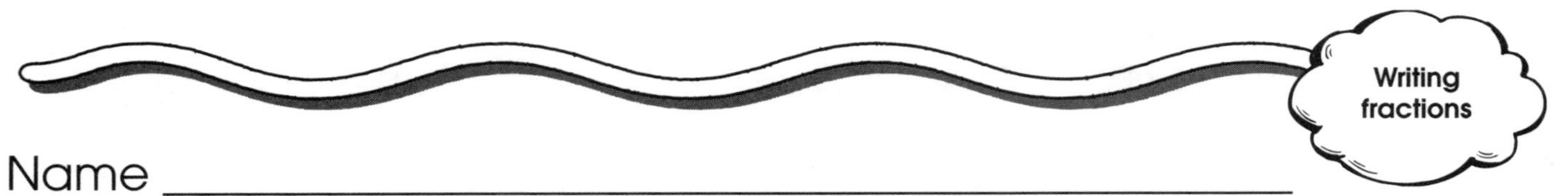

Name ______________________________

Fraction Fun

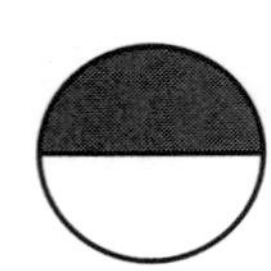

$\frac{1}{2}$ The top number in a fraction tells how many parts are shaded.
The bottom number in a fraction tells how many equal parts.

Write the fraction for the shaded part.

A. 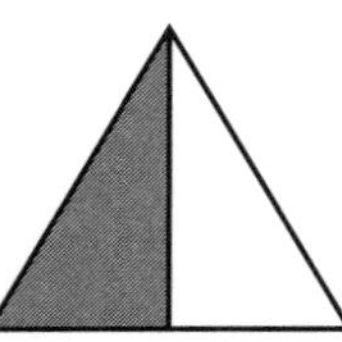 $\frac{\square}{\square}$

B. 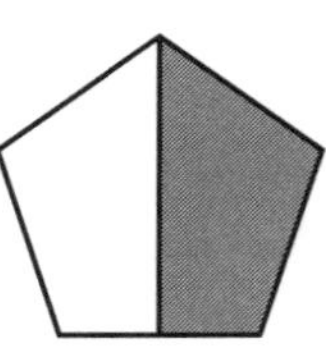 $\frac{\square}{\square}$

C. 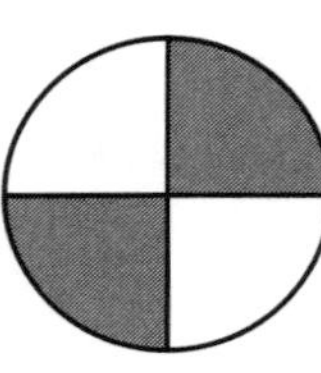 $\frac{\square}{\square}$

D.  $\frac{\square}{\square}$

E. 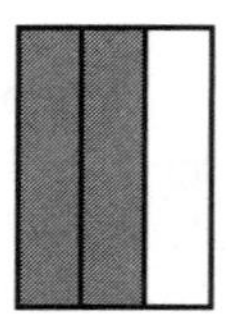 $\frac{\square}{\square}$

F. 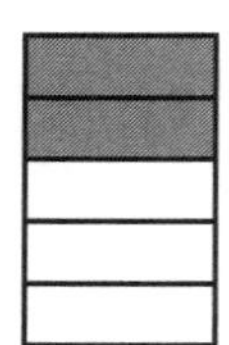 $\frac{\square}{\square}$

G. 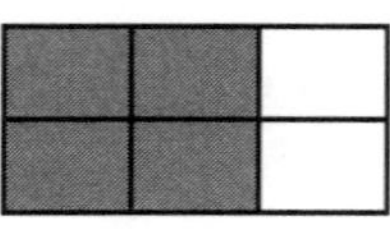 $\frac{\square}{\square}$

H. 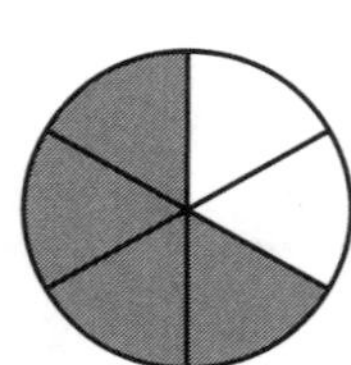 $\frac{\square}{\square}$

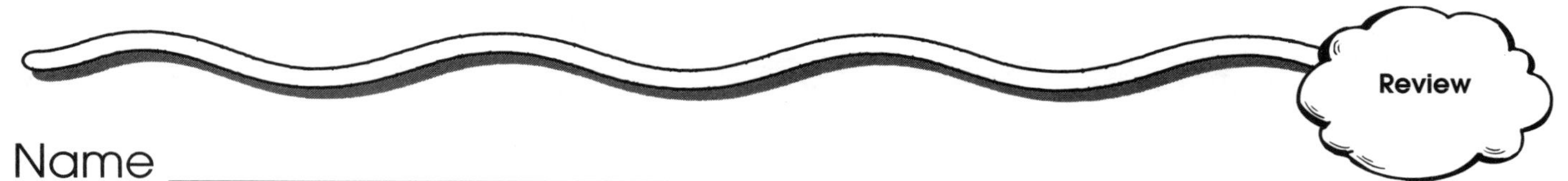

Name ___________________________

Time to Review

Addition and Subtraction of 2- and 3-Digit Numbers, Time and Money, Geometry and Measurement, Graphing and Fractions

Solve.

A. $\begin{array}{r} 96 \\ +\ 12 \\ \hline \end{array}$ $\qquad$ $\begin{array}{r} 215 \\ +\ 168 \\ \hline \end{array}$ $\qquad$ $\begin{array}{r} 45 \\ -\ 18 \\ \hline \end{array}$ $\qquad$ $\begin{array}{r} 489 \\ -\ 317 \\ \hline \end{array}$

Estimate to the nearest hundred and subtract. Then, find the real difference.

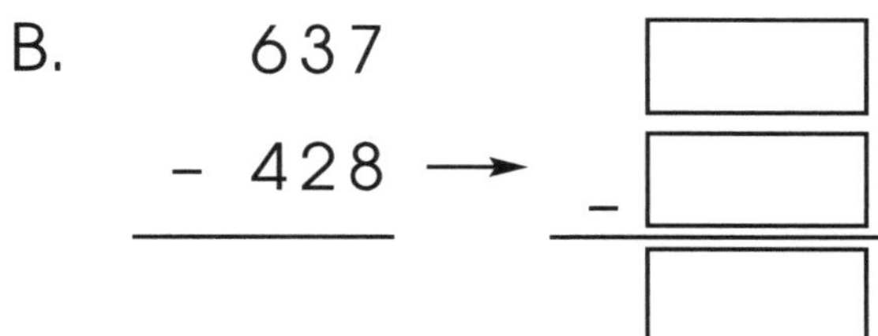

B. $\begin{array}{r} 637 \\ -\ 428 \\ \hline \end{array} \longrightarrow \begin{array}{r} \square \\ -\ \square \\ \hline \square \end{array}$

Find the missing addend.

C. $\begin{array}{r} 3\ 5 \\ +\ \square\square \\ \hline 8\ 9 \end{array}$

Solve.

D. Jim wants to buy a box of crayons for 85¢. Draw coins to show how much he will need.

Name ____

Write a number sentence for each word problem. Solve.

E. There are 84 passengers on the train. At the first stop, 21 passengers get off. How many passengers are left?

F. Mrs. Taylor's class solved 486 math problems in January. They solved 337 math problems in February. How many problems did they solve in all?

Solve the problems.

G. Does a pint hold more or less than a quart? Circle.

more　　　less

H. Write the time that the clock shows.

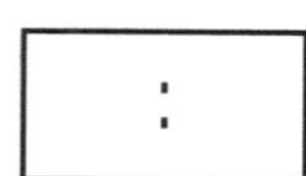

I. Circle the shape that is congruent to .

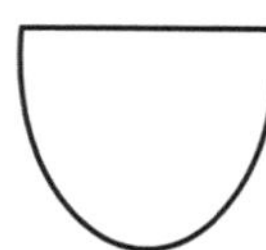

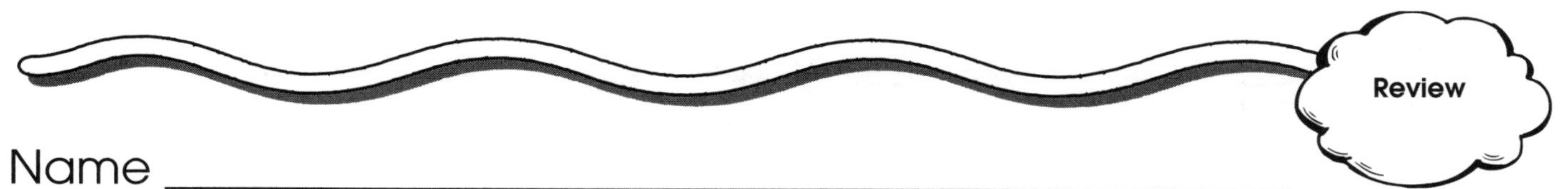

Name ______________________________

J. Find the perimeter of the shape.

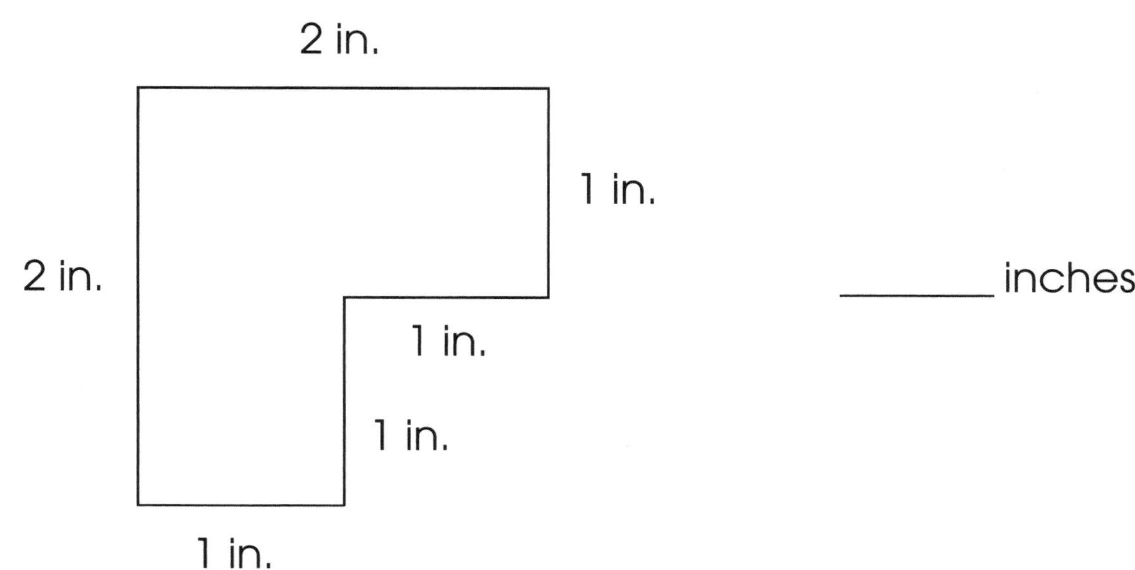

_______ inches

K. Write the fraction for the shaded part.

L. Write the amount.

= _______¢

M. Draw coins to show another way to make this amount.

Answer Key

Page 4
A. 7; B. 11; C. 12; D. 10; E. 14; F. 16; G. 9
Check students' drawings.

Page 5

Page 6

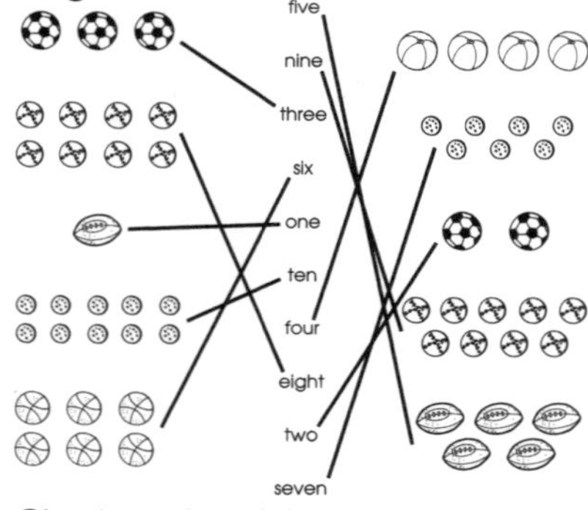

Check students' drawings.

Page 7
Check students' papers.

Page 8
A. 6; B. 14; C. 22; D. 3; E. 20; F. 11; G. 27; H. 7; I. 28; J. 17
The boxes should be placed in the following order: D, A, H, F, B, J, E, C, G, I

Page 9

Page 10
Check students' charts.

Page 11
A. 4; B. 88; C. 22; D. 16; E. 12; F. 36; G. 63; H. 80; I. 51; J. 42

Page 12

All spaces should be colored. The dog reaches the snowman first.

Page 13
A. 2, 4, 6, 8, 10,12, 14, 16, 18, 20; B. 5, 10, 15, 20, 25, 30, 35, 40, 45, 50, 55, 60

Page 14
Check students' charts.

Page 15
A. 10, 9, 8, 7, 6, 5, 4, 3, 2, 1; B. 2, 7, 6, 8, 7, 6, 5

Page 16
A. 30, 60, 90; B. 70, 60, 50, 40, 30, 20; C. 40; D. 70, 60; E. 60, 40; F. 80, 70, 40; G. 60, 40, 30

Page 17

Page 18

Check students' drawings and answers.

Page 19
A. 9, 8; B. 8,10; C. 9,10; D. 12, 11; E. 6, 7; F. 11, 9
In each box, the group with more candies should be circled.

Page 20

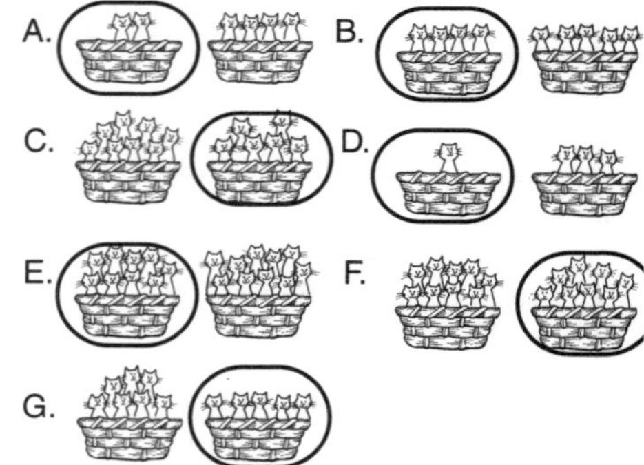

Check students' drawings. Answers will vary.

Page 21

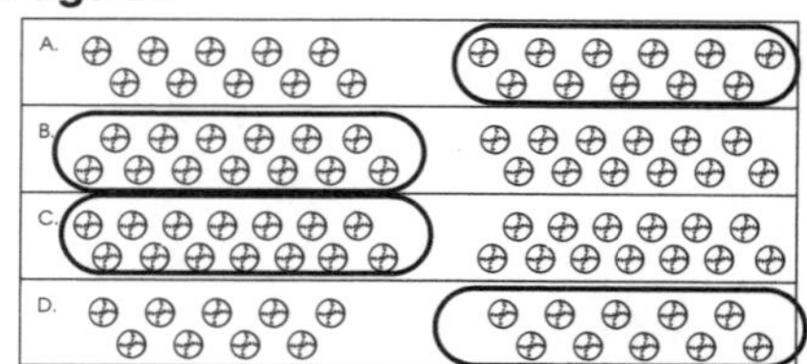

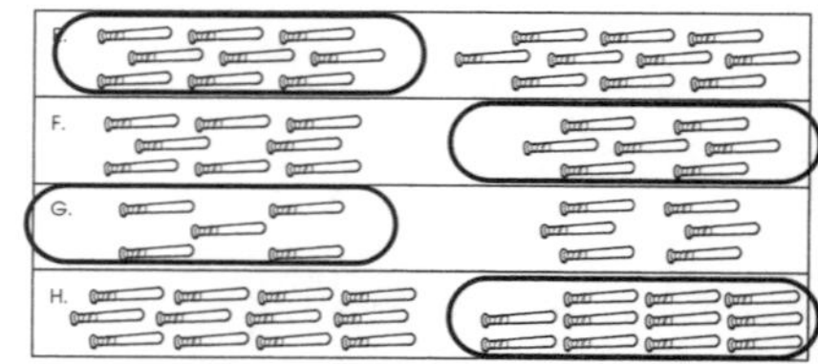

Page 22
A. <; B. >; C. >; D. <; E. >; F. <; G. >; H. >; I. >; J. <

Page 23
A. >; B. <; C. <; D. <; E. >; F. >; G. >; H. <; I. <; J. >; K. >; L. <

Page 24
A. 19, 27, 53; B. 31, 48, 64; C. 12, 25, 36; D. 67, 74, 83; E. 54, 61, 92
Check students' answers. Answers will vary.

Page 25
even numbers less than 28: 8, 10, 14, 24, 26; numbers between 30 and 50: 32, 36, 40, 44, 48; odd numbers greater than 11: 15, 19, 21, 27, 29

Answer Key

Page 26
A. 60, 40, 30; B. 50, 70, 10; C. 90, 50, 80; D. 20, 40, 70

Page 27

Page 28
A. 5; B. 9; C. 6; D. 10; E. 4; F. 9; G. 8; 3 + 4 = 7

Page 29
A. 12; B. 11; C. 10; D. 10; E. 12; F. 12; G. 11; H. 11

Page 30
A. 10; B. 14; C. 12; D. 10; E. 14; F. 12; G. 9; H. 13; I. 11; J. 8; K. 14; L. 11; M. 9; N. 11; O. 7; P. 11

Page 31
A. 10, 12, 11; B. 10, 14, 13; C. 11, 9, 13; D. 14, 14, 7; E. 12, 9, 13

Page 32

	5 + 5 = 10	4 + 3 = 7	8 + 7 = 15	2 + 6 = 8
7 + 7 = 14	3 + 7 = 10	9 + 1 = 10	9 + 8 = 17	4 + 5 = 9
8 + 8 = 16	5 + 3 = 8	6 + 4 = 10	9 + 9 = 18	2 + 7 = 9
5 + 6 = 11	7 + 3 = 10	2 + 8 = 10	3 + 8 = 11	7 + 9 = 16
7 + 8 = 15	1 + 9 = 10	9 + 6 = 15	7 + 4 = 11	
9 + 6 = 15	4 + 6 = 10	8 + 2 = 10	5 + 5 = 10	

Page 33
A = 11; I = 17; A = 16; S = 7; R = 10; M = 14; M = 15; T = 6; N = 12; A = 8; L = 13; W = 9; O = 18; L = 5; MARTIAN–MALLOWS

Page 34
A. 10, 14, 8, 4, 7; B. 12, 11, 15, 6, 14; C. 17, 4, 7, 10, 5; D. 9, 10, 13, 18, 5; E. 15, 11, 16
Check students' addition problems. Problems will vary.

Page 35

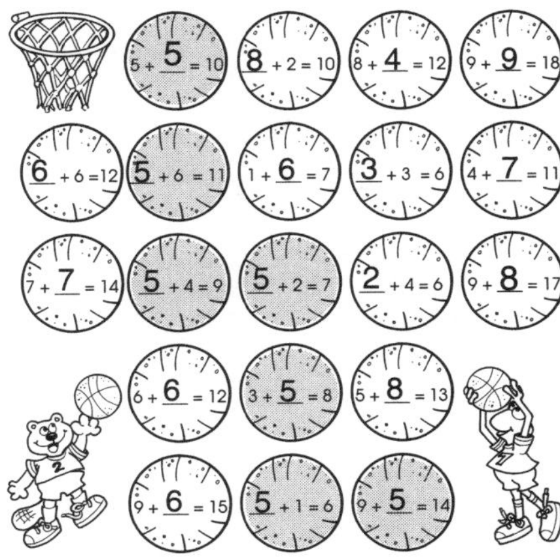

The frog basketball player (#7) made the winning basket.

Page 36
Circled numbers will vary.
A. 12, 16, 13, 11; B. 14, 13, 9, 11; C. 12, 17, 11, 13

Page 37
A. altogether; 5 + 4 = 9; B. altogether; 3 + 8 = 11; C. in all; 2 + 5 = 7; D. in all; 6 + 7 = 13

Page 38
A. 8 + 6 = 14 balls; B. 6 + 4 = 10 games; C. 9 + 5 = 14 marbles; D. 3 + 9 = 12 laps; E. 7 + 4 = 11 goals; F. 8 + 5 = 13 minutes

Page 39
The correct number of cookies in each jar should be crossed out.
A. 3; B. 2; C. 0; D. 2; E. 2; F. 2; G. 3; H. 3

Page 40
The correct number of items in each backpack should be crossed out.
A. 4, 5, 6, 5; B. 3, 4, 1, 6; C. 2, 3, 5, 0

Page 41
A. 6, 6, 9; B. 9, 6, 6; C. 6, 4, 2, 7; D. 9, 1, 7, 9; E. 7, 3, 5, 5; Four flowers were left.

Page 42
A. 12 – 4 = 8, 14 – 7 = 7, 10 – 3 = 7; B. 13 – 8 = 5, 6 – 3 = 3, 9 – 5 = 4; C. 11 – 5 = 6, 14 – 6 = 8, 8 – 8 = 0
Check students' subtraction problems and drawings. Problems will vary.

Page 43
A. 4, 6, 5, 8, 0, 7, 9, 1; B. 2, 3, 8, 9, 6, 5, 7, 4
The pig splashes into the water first.

Page 44
A. 14 – 7 = 7; B. 8 – 5 = 3; C. 15 – 6 = 9; D. 18 – 9 = 9; E. 13 – 8 = 5; F. 11 – 4 =7; G. 9 – 3 = 6; H. 16 – 5 = 11; I. 17 – 9 = 8; J. 12 – 2 = 10
Check students' subtraction problems. Problems will vary.

Page 45
A. 8, 3, 1, 9, 6, 4, 9, 3; B. 2, 0, 7, 9, 8, 4, 8, 1; C. 4, 3, 7, 9, 2, 8, 5, 5; D. 5, 6, 1, 4, 2, 6

Page 46
A. 11, 11, 6, 5; B. 12, 12, 4, 8; C. 15, 15, 8, 7; D. 17, 17, 9, 8; E. 9, 9, 6, 3; F. 13, 13, 6 + 7 = 13, 6, 13 – 6 = 7

Page 47
A. have left; 8 – 3 = 5; B. How many more; 10 – 5 = 5; C. How many more; 9 – 6 = 3; D. have left; 12 – 6 = 6

Page 48
A. 15 – 8 = 7; B. 10 – 5 = 5; C. 12 – 8 = 4; D. 18 – 9 = 9

Page 49
A. 7 + 9 = 16 lizards; B. 12 – 5 = 7 bees; C. 8 – 7 = 1 ant; D. 6 + 4 = 10 turtles; E. 16 – 8 = 8 frogs

Page 50

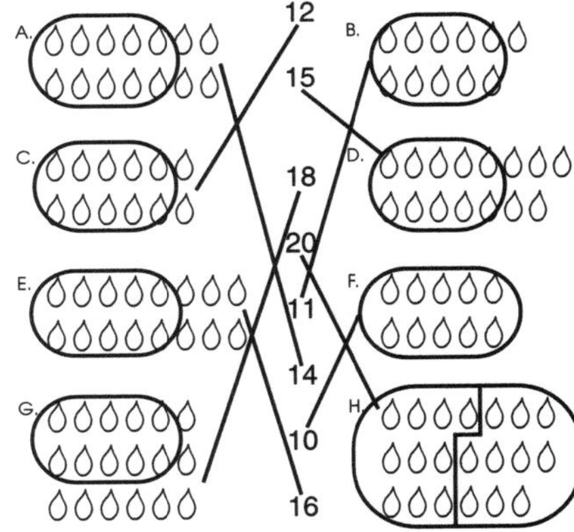

10, 11, 12, 14, 15, 16, 18, 20

Page 51
A. 2 tens 5 ones; B. 4 tens 6 ones; C. 4 tens 2 ones; D. 2 tens 9 ones; E. 5 tens 0 ones; F. 3 tens 1 one; G. 3 tens 7 ones; H. 1 ten 8 ones

Answer Key

Page 52

Page 53
A. 54; B. 27; C. 89; D. 75; E. 16; F. 43; G. 60; H. 91; I. 8; J. 32; K. 7 tens 1 one; L. 5 tens 8 ones; M. 0 tens 5 ones; N. 4 tens 0 ones
91, 89, 75, 60, 54, 43, 32, 27, 16, 8

Page 54
A. 45, 28, 64; B. 82, 37, 15; C. 54, 73; D. 35, 20
RECTANGLES

Page 55
A. 44 + 10 = 54; B. 61 + 10 = 71; C. 73 + 10 = 83; D. 18 + 10 = 28; E. 29 + 10 = 39; F. 55 + 10 = 65
72; 43; 97; 15; 66; 31

Page 56
A. 25; B. 49; C. 8; D. 52; E. 60; F. 37

Page 57
A. 325; B. 192; C. 800; D. 408; E. 276

Page 58

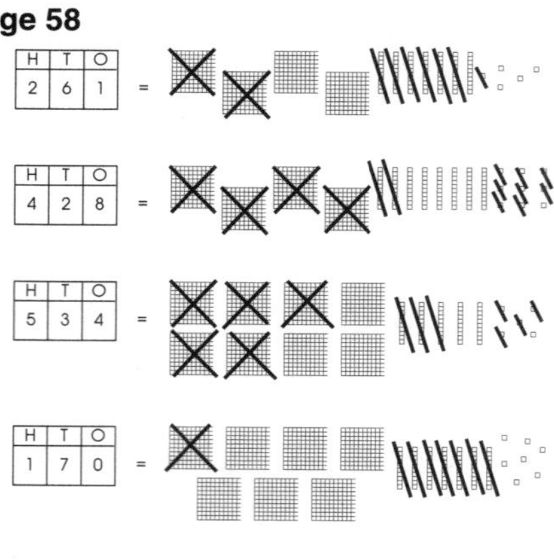

Page 59
A. 253; B. 818; C. 681; D. 366; E. 147; F. 409

Page 60

10

Page 61
A. 12; B. eight; C. 80, 84, 85, 86, 87, 88, 89; D. 32, 31, 30, 29, 28, 27, 26; E. 6, 10, 12; F. 35, 40, 55

Page 62
G. 19; H. 41; I. <; J. >; K. 13, 36, 63; L. 25, 34, 40; M. 18; N. 35; O. 15 – 18 = 7 problems

Page 63
P.

Q. 12, 6, 9; R. 2, 8, 7; S. 10, 8, 12, 13, 7; T. Facts will vary.; U. 46; V. 261; W. 43

Page 64
A. 95, 49, 79, 38, 88; B. 59, 56, 78, 89, 97; C. 86, 96
The bowling pin on the right will fall next.

Page 65
A. =; B. >; C. <; D. =; E. <; F. >

Page 66
A. 13, 14, 52; B. 42, 10, 24; C. 33, 5; Check students' answers. Addends will vary.

Page 67
Across: A. 858; C. 657; Down: A. 876; B. 877; Across: A. 799; C. 945; Down: A. 769; B. 995

Page 68
A. 42; B. 23; C. 34

Page 69
A. 41, 60, 24, 73; B. 33, 91, 82, 51; C. 22, 40, 94, 64

Page 70
A. 94; G. 71; S. 90; F. 93; E. 96; O. 88; I. 77; D. 52; N. 81; L. 65; R. 32
DRAGONFLIES

Page 71
A. 84, 98, 78, 108, 71; B. 72, 30, 111, 74; C. 150, 125, 151; D. 121, 70, 130
The frozen treat on the right will be finished first.

Page 72
A. 73; B. 115; C. 68; D. 105; E. 82; F. 123; G. 126; H. 103; I. 94

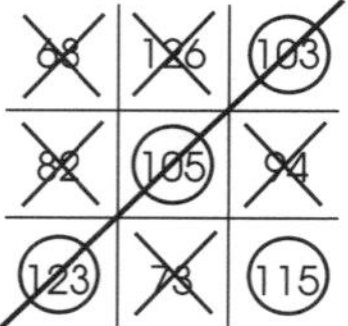

Page 73

Page 74
A. 838, 767, 813; B. 738, 929, 835; C. 747, 909, 859; D. 916, 944, 568

Page 75
A. 840, 871, 807, 520; B. 734, 954, 863, 903; C. 322, 924, 843, 881; D. 961, 432, 751, 930
Check students' answers. Answers will vary.

Answer Key

Page 76

A. 256 + 315 = 571 miles; B. 26 + 17 + 31 = 74 pages; C. 496 + 468 = 964 points; D. 49 + 51 = 100 cars

Page 77

H. 31; I. 52; T. 33; G. 74; P. 15; M. 32; E. 44; O. 10; L. 12; L. 43; H. 53; P. 42; A. 11; N. 24
THE HOPPING MALL

Page 78

A. 412, 732, 243, 385, 321; blue, blue, red, yellow, yellow; B. 564, 402, 152, 645, 321; green, blue, blue, red, yellow; C. 315, 534, 172, 492, 243; yellow, green, blue, blue, red; D. 313, 334, 501, 432, 662; yellow, yellow, green, blue, blue
Check students' subtraction problems. Problems will vary.

Page 79

A. 17, 24, 7, 18; B. 39, 13, 57, 8; C. 19, 15, 27, 46

Page 80

A. 50 – 10 = 40; B. 70 – 30 = 40; C. 70 – 50 = 20; D. 90 – 50 = 40; E. 30 – 20 = 10; F. 50 – 40 = 10; G. 20 – 10 = 10; H. 70 – 20 = 50

Page 81

A. 327, 536; B. 118, 324, 108, 358; C. 206, 246, 26, 317; D. 412, 129, 129, 238; E. 607, 114

Page 82

287, 183, 265, 275, 241, 251, 53, 590, 354, 355, 493, 226, 187, 466

Page 83

A. 263, 461, 138, 586; B. 377, 187, 442, 486; C. 175, 289, 275, 588
Check students' subtraction problems. Problems will vary.

Page 84

A. 600 – 400 = 200, 209; B. 500 – 300 = 200, 234; C. 700 – 400 = 300, 369; D. 900 – 400 = 500, 518; E. 500 – 200 = 300, 374; F. 800 – 700 = 100, 136; G. 400 – 200 = 200, 167; H. 700 – 600 = 100, 145

Page 85

A. 250 – 125 = 125 feet; B. 263 – 127 = 136 inches; C. 43 – 17 = 26 kinds of ants; D. 323 – 291 = 32 pounds

Page 86

A. 102 – 87 = 15 pages; B. 96 + 88 = 184 books; C. 63 + 72 + 48 = 183 minutes; D. 315 – 196 = 119 pages; E. 238 – 197 = 41 words; F. 57 + 125 = 182 books

Page 87

A. 3:00; B. 5:00; C. 7:00; D. 8:00; E.11:00; F. 4:00; G. 9:00; H. 1:00; I. 12:00

Page 88

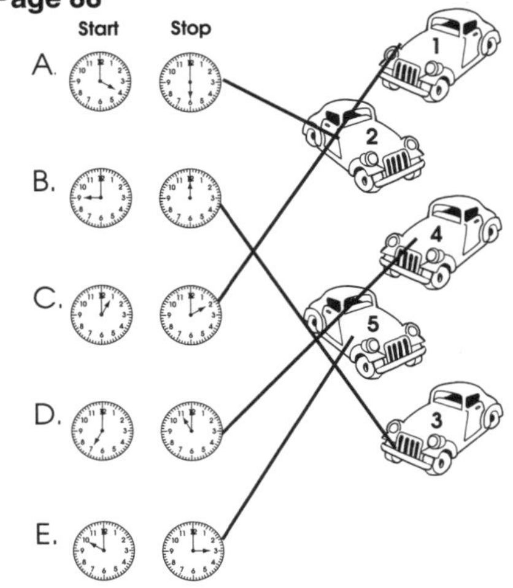

Page 89

A. 3; B. hiking, fishing; C. crafts;
D.

Page 90

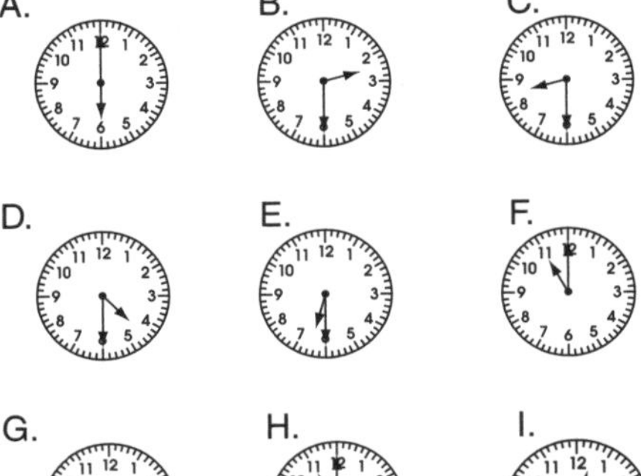

Page 91

Clocks A, B, C, F, G, J, and K should be colored.

Page 92

Check students' estimates and activities. Answers will vary.

Page 93

A. 6¢, 11¢, 8¢; B. 13¢, 25¢, 30¢; C. 15¢, 16¢
Check students' drawings. Answers will vary.

Page 94

A. 2 dimes, 1 nickel, 3 pennies; B. 2 dimes, 2 nickels, 1 penny; C. 3 nickels; D. 3 dimes, 1 nickel, 3 pennies; E. 1 dime, 2 nickels, 3 pennies

Page 95

A. blue; B. red; C. blue; D. red; E. blue; F. yellow; G. yellow; H. red; I. yellow

Page 96

A. 76¢; B. 77¢; C. 59¢; D. 70¢
Check students' drawings. Answers will vary.

Page 97

A. 2; B. 4; C. 10; D. 20
Check students' drawings.

Page 98

A. no; B. yes; C. yes; D. no; E. no

Page 99

A. 95 – 72 = 23¢; B. 85 – 67 = 18¢; C. 63 – 45 = 18¢; D. 92 – 83 = 9¢; E. 99 – 80 = 19¢; F. 75 – 38 = 37¢

Page 100

square dancing!

circle:15; square:18; triangle:10; rectangle:13; oval:15

Answer Key

Page 101
A. cylinder; B. rectangular prism; C. cube; D. cone; E. cone; F. cylinder; G. sphere; H. rectangular prism
Check students' answers. Foods will vary.

Page 102
cone: 1 face; cube: 6 faces; cylinder: 2 faces; rectangular prism: 6 faces; sphere: 0 faces
Check students' answers. Items will vary.

Page 103

A.

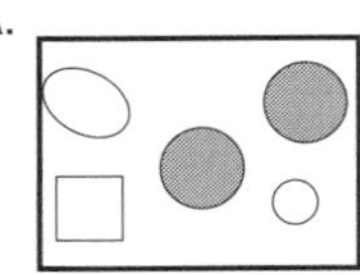

B.

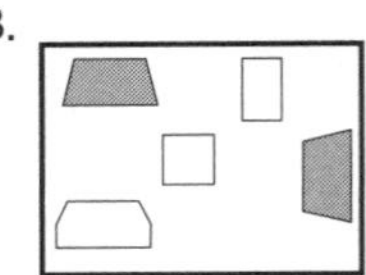

C.

D.

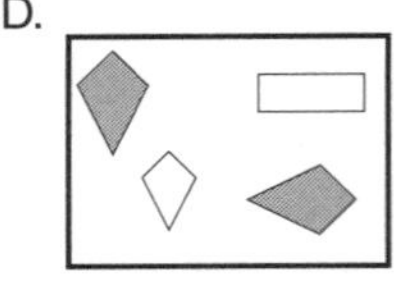

E.

F.

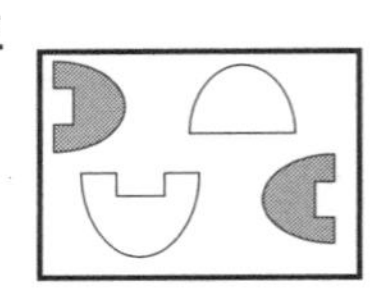

Page 104
A. flip; B. turn; C. turn; D. slide; E. slide; F. flip

Page 105
Check students' drawings.

Page 106
The following should be circled:
A. second cookie; B. third cookie; C. third cookie; D. fourth cookie; E. third cookie

Page 107
A. 3 in.; B. 6 in.; C. 5 in.; D. 4 in.; E. 7 in.; F. 2 in.; G. 1 in.

Page 108
A. 10 cm; B. 12 cm; C. 9 cm; D. 11 cm; E. 8 cm
A WOOF

Page 109
Sam: 1 in.; Marie: 5 in.; Tom: 4 in.; Ning: 2 in.; José: 3 in.; Sandy: 6 in.

Page 110
A. 6 in.; B. 10 in.; C. 8 in.
Check students' answers. Perimeters will vary.

Page 111
A. lighter than one pound; B. heavier than one pound; C. heavier than one pound; D. heavier than one pound; E. lighter than one pound; F. lighter than one pound
Check students' answers. Answers will vary.

Page 112
The following should be colored yellow: mouse, bug, snail, turtle, and bird. The following should be colored blue: penguin, cat, and fox.
Check students' answers. Objects will vary.

Page 113
The following should be colored: A. 2 cups; B. 4 pints; C. 1 quart; D. 4 cups; E. 3 pints; F. 2 quarts

Page 114
The following should be circled: A. fishbowl; B. blender; C. soda bottle; D. thermos; E. lemonade carafe; F. pitcher

Page 115
A. 65° F; B. 50° F; C. 20° F; D. 75° F
Check students' answers. Activities will vary.

Page 116
A. softball; B. four square and ball tag; C. kickball; D. 2

Page 117
A. David; B. 7; C. Carlos; D. 26; E. 6
Check students' answers.

Page 118
A. potato; B. carrot; C. celery; D. broccoli; E. lettuce; F. peas; G. corn; H. spinach

Page 119
J and K should be colored blue; B and H should be colored red; and A, I, and L should be colored yellow.
Check students' answers. Answers will vary.

Page 120
A. 1/2; B. 1/2; C. 2/4; D. 3/4; E. 2/3; F. 2/5; G. 4/6; H. 4/6

Page 121
A. 108, 383, 27, 172; B. 600 – 400 = 200, 209; C. 54; D. Coins will vary.

Page 122
E. 84 – 21 = 63 passengers; F. 486 + 337 = 823 problems; G. less; H. 3:15; I. The first figure should be circled.

Page 123
J. 8 inches; K. 1/4; L. 75¢; M. Coins will vary.